You May Know Them As
Sea Urchins, Ma'am

BREAKWATER

You May Know Them As Sea Urchins, Ma'am

Ray Guy

Selected and Edited by
Eric Norman

Canadian Cataloguing in Publication Data

Guy, Ray.
    You may know them as sea urchins, ma'am

ISBN 0-919519-57-1

I. Title.

PS8563.U9Y68 1985   C818:5402   C85-098680-X
PR9199.3.G89Y68 1985

©1975 Ray Guy
First Printing 1975
Second Printing 1975
Third Printing 1975
Fourth Printing 1976
Fifth Printing 1976
Sixth Printing 1978
Revised Edition 1985

Ray Guy's material reprinted with the kind permission of the original publishers, The Evening Telegram Ltd. (1879-1970) and the St. John's Publishing Company, Limited, publishers for *The Evening Telegram* (1970 –   ).

The Editor wishes to thank Mrs. Mary MacIntyre, Librarian, Gander Collegiate, Gander, Newfoundland, for her services

Breakwater gratefully acknowledges the support of The Canada Council

Cover Photo Hans Weber

Table of Contents

Introduction

I was glad to select, edit and arrange some of Ray Guy's writings for publication.

It was a pleasant task, chiefly because deep affection for his Country pervades most of his work. He often writes in warm blue ink combined with subtle humour and detailed memory to gladden the heart of the reader.

In much of the material I've selected you will find Guy's glances into the past. In these he allows us the luxury of nostalgia, but reminds us of the reality of what was.

He is selective for us. He uses our ears, our eyes, and all our senses as we journey back through the years. He stimulates our own memories as we read, so that we get the double benefit of the reading and the reflection of the reading. He moves us in many places to acknowledge that that is the way it was.

Ray's love for his Country and pride in its past are contagious. He helps us to be proud of those things which yesterday might have made us feel shame. His writing reflects true and rich feelings.

In many ways Guy can be one's conscience. He dares us to be more than we thought we ever could be. He strips the blinkers from our eyes and says - see, there is something noble and strong and valuable in our people, and in our Country. These do not need transformation in order to be of value. The Country is great and beautiful and worthy of praise.

Ray Guy strips the garb of artificial respectability and superiority from some of those who have been set in authority over us. He uses a yardstick different from the ordinary to take the measures of men, and different criteria to judge the value of a way of life.

While his concerns may appear parochial and seemingly of passing importance, his themes are often universal and timeless, and his style will always have charm. For some his writings may be difficult to interpret, but all will find it easy to enjoy him.

During the past year I have read and reread much of what Ray has written since 1968. Much of this writing was done under pressure of a daily deadline. Yet scattered freely throughout are bits and pieces, full columns and groups of lines which catch the eye and the imagination like bright gemstones, or, as he would probably put it, like piss-a-beds in the haygarden. Some of these I have chosen to make this book.

I hope you find enduring pleasure in it.

E.N.
Gander
1975

My Steady Decline into Sin

It all began, I think, when I found out what an ass was.

We were in the ten to twelve-year-old category at the time and a lucky bunch of us had been drilled steadily all that summer preparatory to the laying on of hands.

I still have my copy of the Book of Common Prayer with Hymns Ancient and Modern.

Open it up to the Catechism ("that is to say, an instruction to be learned by every person before he be brought to be confirmed by the Bishop") and the pages are spattered with bug juice.

By God, we were really put through our harness that summer! There's three solid pages of it, for pity's sake, in print even smaller than this, all to be got off by heart.

Some of us were whizzes at it; some were not. Sunday after Sunday we dragged along to school to be exercised in the whole string of questions and answers from top to bottom.

One or two slow learners never did get past the first question. It happens to be, "What is your name?" Thus barred by their deficiency from the bosom of the Established Church they went off and enlisted in the Salvation Army.

After a large quantity of blood, toil, sweat and tears they managed to get me halfway through "My duty towards my Neighbour" before

1

I overflowed at the bung hole with good instruction and could contain not one drop more.

It was a juvenile triumph of sorts. A solid page-and-a-half of catechism off by heart. To mark the occasion I placed a red dot on the spot in "My duty towards my Neighbour" where I had brimmed over.

The last phrase to be crammed in before the hatches were shut was, funnily enough, "...To order myself lowly and reverently to all my betters...."

Anyway, it was somewhere around the latter part of July when we hit the Ten Commandments.

By this time we had put the Apostles' Creed safely behind us, had disposed of "What did your Godfathers and Godmothers then for you?" and were romping through the Ten Commandments more or less with the bit in our teeth.

Comparatively speaking, of course. Because after that summer of close-order drill I, for one, will be no stranger in hell.

We were down to the tenth at last. The hay had been cut, the harbour was calm, the weather was hazy and hot and the flies buzzed outside the Sunday School window.

The teacher, firm but not cruel, was having us put the finishing touches on the Tenth Commandment.

The drill was this. We had to pop up in turn and name one bit or other of they neighbour's goods and chattels which thou shalt not covet...or otherwise the Lord God Jehovah will put thee into a nasty crump.

"Thou shall not covet thy neighbour's house, thou shalt not covet thy neighbour's wife..." in that order, and so forth.

We had run through our neighbour's house, wife, servant, maid and ox and, clearly, there was only one more item on the census form to be filled in.

This hard lot fell to - we'll call him - Benny. Now Benny was a naturally holy child. He might have been conceived in sin and born in iniquity but he reeked sanctity from every well-scrubbed pore.

He was so naturally holy that he always kept his boots well blackened and he would start to bawl if you looked at him sideways.

But now he was put under a great strain.

His colours were coming and going and it was like pulling teeth.

"Come on, now, Benedict," said the teacher. "Speak up. Speak up.

You have been doing so well so far. Thou shalt not covet...what?"

Benny rose in a semi-crouch and discharged his piece in a final burst of agony.

"Thou shalt not covet thy neighbour's arse!"

What followed was an outrage to the Magna Carta. He received a good clip to the earhole and was forced, on the spot, to surrender ten of his small Sunday School cards which he had been saving to exchange for a large motto suitable for hanging in his bedchamber.

The incident brought the Confirmation Class of 1949 to the brink of mutiny.

For poor Benny had been lashed around the fleet in all innocence and purity.

We were...well, I suppose, "backward" is the only way to describe it...in those days having no access to television or other modern helps to education, never in our wildest dreams had we thought there was also an ass with two ears and four legs on it.

Benny had done his best in time of trial. He actually thought that "arse" was a more genteel, a more reverent, a more pious and holy pronunciation of the term.

"Wicked little creatures!" snapped the teacher and she went into a song and dance which cast grave aspersions on the quality of our breeding and management in the home.

Then she whipped out a copy of "Bible Stories For the Infant Soldier – With Many Beautiful Illustrations" and turned up the relevant picture to show us what our neighbour's ass really looked like.

"There it is," she said, glaring around at us. "An ahwse. A beast of burden much used in Biblical times. Ray! Stop that tittering sir, or you will also be required to learn the entire Collect for Septuagesima!"

It was a bit out of season but darned long.

Anyway, our education had been furthered another notch.

We had discovered another brand of ass and were making the most of it. In fact, in what was grimly called "The Final Ten Minutes" in which we were allowed to unship our crayons and draw whatever we fancied as long as it smacked of religion I knocked together a rough likeness of that beast of burden.

It looked something like a cross between a Torbay nag and a Newfoundland dog so I put a label under it..."Thi Neybours As" and took it home for future reference.

Time indoors hangs heavy on the juvenile head. Prior to TV the growing lad had to invent his own diversions. So all during Evensong that day I was developing some small pastime to be put in use in the kitchen before bed.

I got out my picture of the Biblical beast of burden and laid it conspicuously on the kitchen table.

It was to be my first line of defence at the earliest sign of the back of a hand being raised.

For coarse language of any sort was frowned upon greatly. I was a hardy boy before I would risk a "heck" or "darn" within parental earshot.

Later, having graduated to the "heck" level in the home but to the degree of "hell" outside, I would try to correct myself in mid-flight resulting in such curious hybrids as "helk and "darm".

Anyway, my plan for the evening's sport was to just sit there, heave a sigh, gaze around at the kitchen walls and deliver an off-handed monologue to no one in particular. So I commenced:

"Sigh! I wish I had an ass. Make a nice pet, an ass would. Don't think he'd eat much oats. We could keep him in the stable with the sheep. George says his father is getting him an ass for Christmas. I dare say an ass would be good for hauling wood, too. If I had an...."

I was chopped off in my sins because the parental newspaper was being lowered with ominous slowness.

"You already got one, my lad, and you'll get a few swift cuts across it if you don't knock off that carrying on!"

The Flower Garden

Some small account of the old fashioned Newfoundland "flower garden" may be of interest.

In this day and age there are many kinds of gardens. However, the simple, old-fashioned flower garden is still very much in evidence in many outharbours and, with an increasing interest in the nostalgic and the local, we may yet see urban and suburban gardeners display some interest in it.

We must generalize, of course. The sorts of plants used varied widely from place to place and that subject is worthy of a study in itself. However, we will make some attempt to describe a typical plot.

The "lawn" and therefore the lawnmower were unknown. Any grass under fence around a house was reared as hay and cut and dried about the last of July as feed for cattle during the winter.

But any grass not under fence, that is to say, the neat borders of the gravel roads and lanes, any abandoned plot or meadow or any cliffside paths or corners were kept as finely trimmed as the lawn of the great estate.

Before the motor car appeared in any great numbers to stir up clouds of choking dust, and before the bulldozer and grader were introduced to mangle the ditches and roadsides into stones and mud, these gravel roadsides were picturesque indeed.

The sheep of the community were allowed to roam at large throughout the summer and did the work of a small army of gardeners and groundsmen in keeping all unfenced grassground nibbled as clean as any lawn.

But to return to the garden proper. This was a tightly fenced enclosure of, say, fifteen feet by twenty feet, situated in front of the house facing the road.

It was fenced with palings about four feet in height which were sometimes whitewashed but more often left to weather in the course of five years or so to a natural grey. If there was a gate it was only there for show and was nailed permanently closed.

The front door of the house opened directly into this garden but of course it was never used for entry or exit. On the warmest of summer afternoons it might be left ajar and the air that wafted through was scented with roses and lilacs.

These were the two basic trees in the old-fashioned garden. The lilac bush was extremely hardy and grew very well by the seashore. In communities that have been long abandoned even the houses may have fallen down and their foundations been overgrown by the turf, but every June the lilac bush blooms there still.

Unlike today's more delicate and varied sorts of rose bushes, the standard old rose tree grew to ten or twelve feet in height. It had a short blooming season compared to the modern hybrid teas and floribundas.

The roses were sometimes white, but most often "rose." They were the size of small heads of cabbage and intensely fragrant. A scent is sadly lacking from some modern roses which, although of exquisite form and colour, might just as well be plastic as far as the nose is concerned.

A clump or two of orange lilies, a small bed of pansies, a few roots of bleeding hearts, an edging of ribbon grass were some of the other plants in the garden. There might also be the golden balls which resemble giant buttercups, and a bunch of ostrich feather which had purple-blue flower spikes something like delphiniums.

All these hardy and simple sorts of ornamentals required very little care. Only two or three times a season did the gardener have to cultivate or add fertilizer and dig out any encroaching grass.

A few other plants were found in the front garden such as the one called tansy which was used in a homemade remedy and chives (pronounched scyves) which were employed in cooking, plus caraway, the seeds of which were used in baking.

At the back of the house one might find hop vines climbing up to the low eaves, or a gooseberry bush by the corner. All in all, the old fashioned garden was a simple and easy-to-manage affair. Yet the total effect of it in late June was immensely comforting to view as many Newfoundlanders will recall.

The neatly nibbled border of grass between the road and the weathered paling fence, the old roses tumbling out through the palings, the path leading around to the back door, the steeply pitched roof with its grey shingles, the small-paned windows glimpsed through the branches of the lilac bush....

It all sounds too much like the watercolour pictures in some old book of verse to be true, yet readers may agree that it is an accurate sketch of a typical house and garden in many of our outharbours not so long ago.

On the Neck

How clever were our fathers to place their gardens on the "necks" in days gone by!

Two good reasons occur to me for their choosing these sandy necks of land which form barrisways with a brackish pond on one side and the salt water on the other.

The sun, you see. Sometimes a scarce commodity here in fair Terra Nova. But consider such a neck running north and south. In the morning such sun as there was glanced for a few hours off the bosom of the pond, let us say, into the vegetable leaves on the neck with both the power of the real sun and that of its reflection.

And in the afternoon the same phenomenon of the double sun from the seaward side – and who has felt the afternoon sun glancing from the face of the ocean through the kitchen window and does not know its double power thus achieved?

How clever were our fathers to perceive this and give their vegetables the benefit of four suns a day! Did they discover it by observation? Was it transmitted in the horticultural lore of the Old Country? Who can say?

Fencing could be got to these necks by boat, the easiest way possible, and neck gardens were open and bare to the line of sight and could be watched against marauding school youngsters, invading cattle and the runaway, and the stranger bent on thievery.

Convenient the way caplin scull coincided with the trenching of potatoes. Kelp, or as we used to say, "kell-lup" was also employed.

And manure.

Some of my happiest remembrances of childhood are connected with manure.

What joy it was, for example, to be allowed to sit upon a box cart of hen's manure behind our pony, old Nick, on a warm day in spring and rattle over the dusty gravel road to our garden.

Yes, incredible isn't it, that a dollop of that substance which in these crude times is referred to as chicken asterisk can still elevate one to such nostalgic heights.

But cow manure was indubitably considered the best. It was said to have more substance, body and "virtue" than any other. It was the crème de la crème of mammalian dung.

Next in point of desirability came sheep manure. It stank more and it was devilishly hard to hack that foot-thick layer out of the stable in springtime as it tended to mat.

But if set aside to age in a pile for twelve months it was magic in the potato patch. Ambrosia to the turnips, an epicurian treat for the carrots, beets and other "small fruits" as the old people called them.

Horse manure was pretty worthless, or considered so. It was said to have hardly any of this indefinable quality, "substance", at all. It was useful in hotbeds if anyone wanted to go to that trouble but otherwise would be scattered around the grass ground just to get rid of it.

The trouble with hen's manure was that it was thought to be too strong. If slung on too fresh and in any amount it burned up the vegetables. But if rotten and used sparingly it was good enough.

Cleaning out a hen's house is a pretty good test of the respiratory system. Because of the ammonia in it, it is sharp as and breath-taking as a bottle of Minard's Liniment.

The caplin pit, moving with little white maggots, or the fishes guts pit in a like condition, was a useful source of nutrient for the potatoes.

Some people used to put what is now called "human excrement" on their gardens as manure. But as I recall, this was seen, even in those days, as a primitive measure.

I don't know why. The clever Japs have been doing it for years. And don't we pay a good price today for processed human excrement as provided by the folk of Chicago, Ill.?

9

At any rate, thus manure. How times flies. I can't get over it.

I can remember old Nick flicking his ears and switching his tail and chewing on a bit of clover as the box cart behind him was dumped of hen's manure onto the ground.

After all that tender loving care there's no grass on the spot now. They've built the new school over it. Still lots of manure, eh, chaps, but not the sort that makes the grass grow.

Assassins in the House

I took the news badly.

"Take that, you villain!" I cried, fetching the gleaming soul of treachery a telling blow with a sixteen-pound maul hastily brought up from the cellar.

"Oh, that I have harboured such a viper," I exclaimed, putting redoubled heft behind my whacks, "to my bosom for so many years!"

When Mr. Churchill declared war on Japan he observed that "when you are about to kill a man it costs nothing to be polite" but I figured this didn't apply to electric kettles.

Here I relied fully on Scriptures in which we are told "if thy electric kettle offend thee, put thy sandals to it."

Applying a burned-earth policy to discovered fifth-column appliances is an exhausting business.

I gave the battered remains of the insidious assassin a few Kung Fu chops for good measure, then administered the coup de grace by jumping on it with both feet from a kitchen chair.

"Polly, put the kettle on now!" thought I in panting triumph as the cord of the foiled household guerrilla twitched in the final throes and lay forever stilled.

What stung most is that my mother – in all innocence, as I trust – had given me the steaming back-stabber as a present on my birthday.

How quickly the times are moving.

Until the news broke I had always thought that lead poisoning was something to which one succumbed under a little cactus bush on the Arizona desert after vexing Billy the Kid.

Little did I dream of being sent to Boot Hill by a teakettle.

The recollection of it grates. My sympathy towards Herr Brandt of Germany who unknowingly hired a spy for secretary has increased by leaps and bounds. How many times have I, thinking there might be germs in the well water, boiled it in that accursed implement for the sake of hygiene!

We now wait with trepidation for the authorities to publish the symptons of teakettle lead poisoning.

Whatever they are I'm sure I have them. A certain heaviness in the bottom of the stomach these past months, a dull, leaden (O, the unconscious irony of it!) sensation in the head, an odd notion that one's boots have mysteriously increased in weight...and all that.

Two cups of coffee at breakfast plus the occasional dish of tea in the evening...over the years this all adds up.

With such an accumulation of lead in the system I know what I'm up against. I have cancelled all plans for a holiday. Hedged by uncertainty, I'm sure only that it'll take more than the usual six pallbearers to lug my overweighted box along to the graveyard.

Of course, if the kettle hadn't got me there's a myriad of other household assassins as would have.

I remember the time, early on in the days of consumer protection, that stark terror reduced me to a straight diet of mustard pickles.

Warnings were coming thick and fast. There was a steady bleat on the CBC radio and in the more conscientious journals about newly-discovered victuals that were but little slower than strychnine taken neat, and much more certain.

When it was revealed that beef cattle were being injected with the most appalling sorts of hormones I went off it in a flash. But no sooner had I taken to fowls than I was informed they were fed on provender laced with arsenic to keep them alert and bushy-tailed.

For a short while fish was my only dish until the mercury thing came to light after which I went vegetarian. I was no sooner used to three squares on herbs and lentils when the news came out that the vegetables were merrily dosed with enough sprays to knock down hardy rats at fifty paces.

I was headed for the woods determined to get away from it all and eat nothing but caribou steaks for what little time I had left when the radioactive lichens revelations came out.

Your average caribou, it had been discovered, has no better amusement than to stand around muching lichens – one of nature's best storehouses of radioactive fallout.

It was at this time that I tried to subsist on mustard pickles.

Just then one of the more avant garde journalists wrote that pickles are preserved by the same substance used to embalm corpses.

This was a low point in my career. I was rapidly losing weight and my nerves commenced to go. In an effort to salvage the latter I started taking regular doses of Bromo-Seltzer.

One day as I was belching about the house the radio informed me that one of Bromo-Seltzer's ingredients, phenacetin, had been proved a kidney-rotter capable of rendering whole hutches full of rabbits joyless.

Well, Bromo-Seltzer is still on the open market, I notice, and so, through the grace of God and the intercession of the Holy See, am I.

But failing fast and, having been sabotaged for years by a treacherous kettle, standing in slight hopes of hanging up my stocking next Christmas.

As a consumer, I have fallen prey to just about every peril that has come down the turnpike.

Whisker dust from electric shavers could cause lung cancer I learned only a fortnight after getting one for graduation.

I used to eat maraschino cherries straight out of the jar before it was announced that the red dye used in them had caused fallen arches in some convicts in Idaho.

Just as I started saving for a colour television set the word came out that the radiation from one could roast you like a kipper if you dozed off in front of it.

Although fortified to know that fat persons survive longer if they fall through the ice, I took the experts' warnings about overweight to heart and drank gallons of diet drinks before the terrible tidings about cyclamates struck.

It has been an unrelieved nightmare. The little old ladies who claim that fluoridation of the water supply is a Communist plot to wipe out the western world must be daft. Why should the Communists bother?

13

For the past few weeks there's been a steady bulletin from the CBC consumer protection bellwethers concerning the perils of a certain brand of black pepper.

I, for one, am tired of running. I'm going to buy another electric kettle, get a good stock of black pepper and drink boiled water spiked with pepper until merciful release is achieved.

And then they can embalm me in mustard pickles, bury me in a colour television set, and sprinkle marachino cherries on my grave.

Landwash

Let us turn aside for the nonce from the hurly-burly of today's world and dip into those comprehensive volumes of nostalgia, Guy's Encyclopedia of Juvenile Outharbour Delights.

We pick at random Volume Six and flip open to page 74 where we see described the process of "Arsing Around Down in the Landwash".

Here is a definitive treatise on a mysterious world which is familiar ground to every juvenile with access to it, but which seems to have been either forgotten or dismissed by an adult population.

Wherever the salt water breaks in against the edge of the dry land you will see there a common meeting place for juveniles who find themselves in the vicinity.

I think this is a world-wide law of nature. Latitude has nothing to do with it. Where there is a landwash, be it in Arnold's Cove or in Indonesia, there will the juvenile inhabitants congregate regularly.

It is a magnet to the younger rural set. It has to do with age. Whereas the juvenile sees it as a complete and infinitely fascinating place, adults dismiss it as "a damned old beach" with a few rusty cans and trash on it.

Anyway, this is how it used to be.

Funnily enough, your outharbour juvenile had no conception of tides until much later in life.

This is odd as, domiciled where he was, the tide made higher – as was the saying – and the tide made lower a couple of times each twenty-four hours within half a gunshot of his house.

But it did not enter into his head that there was a regularity to it, and certainly not that the moon and the sun in the sky had anything whatsoever to do with it.

It was a fresh discovery each day. A member of the party would happen to glance seaward during the course of other juvenile activities and observe that, by gracious, the water was now low.

Here was another completely automatic reaction. If the water was low it seemed to be programmed into the outharbour juvenile's consciousness that the only sensible thing to do was to make for the landwash.

There are many laws and regulations which cement the adult world together in rough fashion. Basic things such as not breaking wind in polite society or allowing each person a vote apiece on polling day.

Similarly, a law prevails in the outharbour juvenile world that if the water is low there is only one regulation above the world, the flesh and the devil – on noticing the fact, all concerned must go down to the beach.

Once there, the most crystal clear obvious thing to do is go "arsing around".

These are decadent times. We have just about lost our language along with everything else. Such a phrase has to be explained in a most demeaning way.

But we learn to live with "musts". Some English person wrote a phrase to the effect that "there is nothing half so good as messing around in boats." Everyone knows it.

However, we don't mess around in this poor corner of the world. In Newfoundland we "arse" around.

Hence, arsing around down in the landwash.

Enough of the mechanics of the exercise and down to the fine point of it.

Turning over rocks is the principal activity.

The purpose of turning over rocks is manifestly clear to all but adults and prairie farmers. You turn over rocks to see what is under them. Otherwise, how would you know?

There are crabs under rocks. Sometimes when you turn over a

rock a crab will rush off and crawl under another rock. This places on you the responsibility of turning over that rock, yes, and five more if Mr. Crab won't stop steady.

You catch them and put them into crocks. Catching a crab is no easy matter. It is the heights of hyprocrisy for older persons to tell youngsters that crabs - and emmets too - won't bite you.

It's a lie. A crab can bite you. It can bite you on the finger very hurtfully and make it bleed and perhaps all your blood will run out...if you don't know the proper way of holding it.

However, your outharbour juvenile is well versed and knows the ins and outs of things. I suppose he picked it up from his slightly older colleagues on the landwash. Picking up crabs without bleeding is child's play.

You have to be smart about it. There is only one place to grab them. I won't detail the method in case persons of impressionable years will be tempted to experiment and get injured by a crab which injury would then be on my conscience.

There is no way you can learn about it without being an outharbour juvenile with some slightly older colleague to tell you how.

Once, however, you know how to do it you can go on to pick up lobsters and every other thing under the sun without getting bit. If you think this is lies, Mrs. Aunt Milly Hynes out home could pick up a vicious dumbledore in her bare fingers, easy as pie, and not get stung.

There! Put that in your pipe and smoke it! There are a lot of thing you don't know yet.

Anyhow, you catch crabs and put them into crocks. Some will say what is the purpose of this. Well, the purpose is to see how many you can catch, pure and simple.

When someone further along asks you how many you have cotch so far you can say seven or eight and one big one, as the case may be, and then they give you a report on their own collection.

Carbs is nice but next on the list is tansies.

You put them in a crock, too. They are scarcer than crabs but, to the best of my knowledge, tansies can't bite.

I don't want to spend the rest of my life explaining what different things are. There is a limit to anyone's patience. But a tansie is a small thing like an eel, brown on the back and yellowish sort of on the gut, and they are under rocks, too.

17

Also you will find your swimps. This is what is called "shrimps" in the Boston States. To hell with that as once you cross the Gulf we have charge of naming our own neighbours and they are swimps!

There are swarms of them under the rocks. But they are small and hardly worth the effort of putting into crocks. Still, they are there for anyone to see.

You will get the scattered wassaname into a big wrinkle as well. It is still a "wassaname" as far as the author is concerned. He got to be a hardy boy without hearing the question resolved.

These things are into big wrinkles and are much like a crab in their forward parts. But when you take them out they are almost like a little tiny lobster. Some said they were lobsters and some said they were not. It is left up to the university to say which. Anyhow, they are curious things.

Your outharbour juvenile didn't have names on half the stuff which is under rocks. He used to collect up some wassanames which were exactly the size and shape of a carpenter - everyone knows what a carpenter is - but white.

After such and such a time you'd sit down on a rock and look at your crock full of crabs and things for a spell. Then you'd say, shag this, as the water is getting high again and heave the bottle and all in the water and go about your business. This is what goes on all the time. Even, I suppose, in the present day and age.

A Very Dangerous Practice

It is quite some time since I engaged in the Outharbour Juvenile Delight known as "Foundering Cliffs".

I got a chance to do so again at Bonavista recently.

There are two methods for the proper foundering of cliffs. One is where you get down on the beach and keep chucking up rocks at a piece of cliff that is loose and almost ready to fall.

Presently, it is dislodged and crashes down in a cloud of dust with quite an amusing roar.

The other method is to get up on top of the cliff and dislodge a loose piece either by chucking rocks at it, poking it with a long stick, or, most trepid of all, getting someone to hold on to your arm while you reach down and kick it with your foot.

This will sometimes start an avalanche down the face of the cliff and the mightly roar and fuss connected with this is quite thrilling and wonderful.

We were walking along the cliffs at Bonavista, the photographer and I, going in the direction of Spillers Cove and Lancaster as he wanted to get closer to a really stupendous rock sticking up off one of the points.

Due to the lie of the land, we walked miles past this picturesque geographical feature without realizing it. The cliffs became much higher.

19

The photographer halted here, but I walked on ahead, determined to find this remarkable rock which we had seen in the distance from the lighthouse road.

I was standing hundreds of feet above the sea, boats and gleaming white icebergs lay on the distant horizon. Some sort of whale or porpoise kept bursting out of the water away down there and even the gulls were flying below me.

Just then I heard a dull roar in the distance, not unlike thunder. Then another, even louder, like heavy artillery. I looked across and saw that it was the photographer foundering cliffs.

Being thus put in mind of a long-forgotten childhood amusement I joined in. It was only a matter of dislodging one small rock and tons of the cliff top would go crashing down hundreds of feet into the sea.

The noise was awesome. At one particularly successful dislodgement the avalanche was so frightening I found myself running away, just as we did then, thinking that the whole cliff might collapse.

If a parent, lecture your offspring most sternly against this extremely dangerous practice as they could easily be killed while at it. Mine always used to.

A Place in the Country

Newfoundlanders have a great fondness for shacks.

A great profusion of them is maintained in all parts. Those with grander notions call them summer cottages or even lodges but the most common term is still "a shack in the country."

If all the "Bide-A-Wees" and "Twill Do Us's" and "Kosy Nooks" were lumped together on one site it would create a considerable, if motley, town.

Larger places like St. John's or Corner Brook spawn these rustic adjuncts in the greatest number, of course, but even those who live in villages of less than one hundred population maintain shacks a little further up the road as retreats "away from it all."

The Newfoundland penchant for a summer shack is not a recent thing.

It was always there. In former times the shacks were perhaps more shacky. A cut-off oil drum on a box of gravel served as a stove and water was lugged up from the nearest brook or river.

As there was nothing inside worth pillaging the door was never locked.

But these days the shack in the country is an only less elaborate replica of the permanent dwelling in town. Oil heat, running water, electricity, landscaped grounds and a TV antenna.

This grander concept of the summer shack cuts a mighty hole in the original conception of such a place as a retreat and a place for relaxation.

Now there are two lawns to be mowed: one in town sometime during the week and another up in the woods on weekends. Two houses to be painted, two plumbing systems to be maintained, two living rooms to be vacuumed, two roofs to be repaired.

Relaxing in the country is now a strenuous business. With crowding up there in the sticks getting worse the change of scene is not now very much of a contrast. Still, Newfoundlanders cherish their summer shacks and the time they can spend in them.

The tender care given to them, the most uninhibited imagination given to their design and decoration, the joy at opening the front door for a weekend often exceeds that shown to the main town dwelling.

It would be too much to say that Newfoundlanders are more frantic for their summer shacks than are other races.

But, in proportion, the enthusiasm here is remarkable.

Outsiders (from St. John's or North Sydney) might think it comical that, for instance, some residents of Clarenville are eager to flee the metropolitan hurly burly of that great city for the serenity of Thorburn Lake.

Or that many inhabitants of that urban jungle, Grand Bank, maintain escape hatches up the road toward Marystown. Persons from Glenwood or Trepassey might be amused that some Townies' idea of being up in the woods is Topsail Pond.

It is interesting to note that the great majority of summer shacks are located, not on the seacoast, but as much inland as possible.

If there's a choice, the preference is always for "up in the country", be it only half a mile from the shore. The swampy, mosquito-ridden pond has it over the noble marine prospect every time.

Of course, it is the change of scene that is paramount. As most of the larger settlements are around the coast, this sort of scenery is open to view most of the year. The change comes with withdrawing from the sight of it.

Another change from tradition in the long-range is that once upon a time the season of the shack in the country was not summer but winter.

Hence, the winter tilt. In winter the people drew inland from the sea to tilts or shacks provided for the purpose. This practice was quite sensible and utilitarian.

By moving inland they escaped the howling coastal winds for some sheltered spot of woods by a river. They were nearer to the wood required for heating and cooking and, being sheltered, required less of it.

There was nothing to be done on the sea as it was too rough or frozen over. Removed a few miles to the country they were nearer the wild game so necessary at that time.

We are so nice now as to suppose this was a practice only along the Labrador coast. But it was followed in almost every part of the Island. The relics of such winter villages may be seen all over.

Perhaps today these sites are occupied only in summer. Summer shacks where once stood winter tilts. When the curse of mosquitos is considered, the summer is a less sensible season for retreating inland than is the winter. But such are the times.

It is lovely and wonderful, though, to have a shack in the country. God grant that we may never be so impoverished as to be forced to forego the custom.

And may Providence preserve us against those burgeoning appurtenances of deviltry and torment – the motor tobaggan in winter and the chain saw in summer.

But You Said We Won

A conversation with an older person who passed away in August 1943, out Home:

Do England still stand?

Oh, yes, sir. And our Sovereign sits yet at her castle at Windsor...as they say.

Oh, they never had a boy, then, after.

No, sir. They never had a boy.

Well, we won, then.

Oh, yes, sir. We won. It was a bit ticklish in spots but we made it.

Um. And how was the fish last year? Much got?

Well, yes and no, sir. There was and there wasn't.

There was a good sign on the first of it but it dwindled off. But lobsters were plenty and a good price.

Is there many canning them now besides Manuel and Abby and Henry Alfred?

No, sir. They passed on, you know. They don't can them any more. The ice came last year.

Ice? Come in? Much?

More than was ever seen since back in your time, sir, they said.

I only seen it twice. No, three times. No, it was only twice I seen it. I think it was only twice. No difference. Did Billy last long?

Oh, yes, sir. He rallied after that and he was great and smart and only passed away, I think it was, the year before...no, in the summer...two years before Confederation. They put his pipe and a bottle of rum in the box along with him.

Eh, my son?

His pipe, sir, and a bottle. They put it in with him. It was his wish.

Confederation?

Oh, that came along in 1949. We were joined on to Canada.

Confederation?

Yes, Confederation. Joined on to Canada. It was in 1949. April Fool's Day. You know, upalong. Canada. We were joined on.

You said we won.

But that was the war, sir. This was after. I can't mind too much about it. I was a boy them.

The Commission done it.

I don't think so, sir, altogether. I'm going by what I'm told. I believe we were more or less on our own again, then.

Then how many was there killed?

So far as I know, sir, there was no one killed. There was only a lot of talk all the time, and swearing. When it came about they put the flag down to half-mast but there was no one killed.

No one?

No, sir. No one...so far as I know.

No one.

The ground is sold, sir, but your house is still there and son John's. They rose the roof on it a long time ago, and they put the water in.

All the flakes are gone now, sir, and they got what they call a fish plant across from the Dock Garden below Uncle Walter's. They don't make fish at all, now, sir.

Do you mind Uncle Walter's saying, sir? "Things will rise and things will fall." I don't sir, but I hear them talk about it.

They say that you and Uncle Abby and Uncle Walter would have something to say if you could only see the television. Or, that's what they used to say first when the television came in.

That's what they said when the men was put on the moon, too. They said you and Uncle Abby and grandfather and them would have something to say about it if you were here now.

It must be hard to believe, sir, all these things. There was a vessel came in through the Bay to the Foxhead last year, sir, longer than The Great Eastern.

They have a thing down there for oil. All the people came down, you know, a few years back, to the Cove. There's nothing up on the Islands now. Wareham's left Harbour Buffett and I was up and saw the church falling down at Merasheen myself.

It must sound wonderful odd to you, sir, but I'm not telling any lies. What, sir?

There wasn't no one killed?

Games Children Play

Whilst I was loitering outside my place of employment the other day endeavouring to solicit from passers-by the price of a bottle of Jordan Valley, I noticed a small disturbance in the alley opposite.

"What ho!" thought I. "Some old age pensioner being relieved of the contents of her handbag, I dare say. Well, no affair of mine, I am sure."

However, the bustle continued for some minutes longer than it generally takes to mug a member of the sunset generation so my curosity was stirred.

Breasting the roar and exhaust fumes of the Duckpuddle Street Grand Prix, I, emulating the chicken, crossed the road and resumed loitering on the corner of the alley.

I perceived immediately that the fuss up this municipal playground was being created by juveniles, the nasty little brutes, but what it was they were doing puzzled me for the nonce.

But I soon caught on. They were up to a most curious game....

"Less play house."

"OK. I'll be the daddy, Lester, and you be the mommy."

"No, I was the mommy last time, Charlene. You got to be the mommy and Rodney and Lisa and Dwight and Todd and Monique can be the children and Terri can be the uncle and Jacquie can be the grandmother and...."

"Naaaa," said the obnoxious brat yclept Rodney, "shucks on that kind of house. Lisa always bawls too much when we comes to the pretend. Less play the other kind of house."

Here occurred a tremendous hubbub for a few minutes, during which the insufferable little beasts debated the pros and cons.

Finally, as best I could make it out, they settled on "the other kind of house."

There was much scuffling and to-do for a few more minutes as these infant prodigies set the scene for their frolic. Finally the jug-eared child, Monqiue, spoke.

"This house will now come to order. Sit down and shut up, all hands. I'm not takin' no lip. I'm Missus Speaker and what I says goes, see?"

"Missus Speaker," pipes Lester, the juvenile most subject to a running nose. "I got some bills here to bring in. These bills is for the party last week. If them liars on the other side of the House says anything about it I'll chop off their heads with an acts."

"Order, order, order," says Monique banging on her orange crate with two foot of hockey stick. "Shut up or you gets a smack in the mouth. I'll get the Left Handed Governor to put you all in jail!"

"Yaaa, yaaa, yaaa. Shut up prissy face or I'll jump the guts out of your dolly next time you comes to our house," responded Lester. "I can bring some bills if I wants to because I'm the Leader of the Obstetrician. Haaaa!"

"Shut up, shut up. Sit down, sit down," observed Dwight with the missing molars, "We got more bills than they got because we had a better party. You better not listen to them, Missus Speaker, because I'm the Preemare and I won't give you none of the money if I don't want to."

"Order!" screeched Monique. "Order!"

"Shut up, numb nut," bawled both the Preemare and the Leader of the Obstetrician in unison.

"Missus Speaker," said a voice from the rear. "I wants to make a movement."

"Well you can't make no movement now," ruled Monique. "We can't have no movements on the floor once the estimates is started. The Honourable Mender should have thought about that before."

"Missus Speaker!" shouted Lester in some heat. "You better watch it or I'll jump on your pencil box. If my Honourable Colic wants to make a movement there isn't no one going to stop him."

"Shame, shame!" cried some Honourable Menders from benches opposite. "Bullies, bullies. Big bullies."

"Order or you all gets a bat in the face," said Missus Speaker impartially. "Rules is rules and we got to stick to them."

"Yes," observed the Leader of the Obstetrician, scornfully, "one lot of rules for them and another lot for us. Ha!"

"Point of odour, Missus Speaker. Point of odour," shouted gap-tooth Dwight, the Preemare. "That shirt-head shouldn't be allowed to say stuff like that. You 'spose to suspend him."

"Missus Speaker! Missus Speaker!" shouted his nemesis at this juncture. "My Honourable Colic wants to make a movement and by jing he got to make one."

"Order or someone's ears is going to smart," ruled Missus Speaker after some consultation of Beauchesne. "The Honourable Mender for Rawlins Cross got the floor."

"I wants to make a movement, Missus Speaker, but I sooner go up around the corner. I got the flu and my mommy said...my mommy said if I got me pants dirty again she was going to lace me."

"Point of odour, Missus Speaker, point of odour!" bawled some Honourable Mender in objection to some scurrilous remarks from Hon. Colics opposite.

By this time the Honourable Mender for Rawlins Cross had beat a hot foot up around the corner, leaving his seat without the usual formalities and nearly bowling over the Surgeon at Alarms.

"Less all go up and peep at him," suggested Missus Speaker addressing the House in general. "Then we'll fire gravel at him and make him run."

This suggestion received the unanimous approval of the Letters Later and all the Honourable Menders pussyfooted in a body, with many a snicker and giggle, to the rear of the alley for a squint at the unfortunate but popular tribune for Rawlins Cross.

Well I can tell you!

I had long admired today's juvenile race for its precocity but these particular specimens astonished me altogether.

It seems likely - although I am not sure - that they had been to the House of Assembly on some school trip or other and were basing their childlike game on experience.

Quite crude their version of what goes on in the Honourable House was, to be sure, and entirely unlike the actual proceedings in point of substance.

But I thought it quite remarkable the way they had managed to grasp the rules or basic formalities of parliamentary procedure for all that.

Police Strike!

A shudder ran down my back on first receipt of the news that the constabulary had gone on strike. Obviously there would be an immediate breakdown in law and order and all that that entails.

No police. No restraints. Anarchy. Back to the jungle. As chance would have it I was sitting in the newsroom when the news arrived. All the more reason to shudder.

I noted an immediate change in my own attitudes. I was out of cigarettes and at that moment one of the slighter communications clerks (they used to be called copy boys in the days when you could send them out for coffee) passed by.

A lawless thought flashed into my mind. How easy it would be, I thought, to stick out a foot, trip the little beggar, snatch his ciggies, and be on the next plane for Rio before he came to.

I attempted to borrow a nylon stocking from one of the desk editors to haul over my head as a disguise. But she was wearing the more modern garment and the pause which ensued gave me time to wrestle with my conscience.

It also allowed me time to give thought to my own situation. Now that the police were on strike I, like everyone else, was open to naked aggression.

If such acts of lawlessness could occur to me, what mischief might be going through the minds of people around me – chaps who perhaps flunked out of Sunday School even worse than I did.

I glanced about. Reporters and editors alike were making furtive movements. Their eyes were narrowed. They knew. There I was with a sum of money and valuable papers on my person. A total of $3.76, in fact, and a receipt for two orders of fish and chips.

Slowly, very slowly, I looked around for some means of defence. I found just the thing in the office of the chief librarian in the shape of a heavy hardwood table leg.

So I sat with my back to a corner and the weapon across my knees determined not to give up my valuables without a scuffle. The situation gave me a new slant on nuclear weapons stockpiling. It was a crude defence but it would have to do until the next day when I could obtain and strap on a pair of six-shooters.

Violence in the streets should be breaking out around now as the news of the police strike spread. I looked out the window unto Duckpuddle Street and sure enough, a little old lady with a shopping bag emerged from the bank across the way.

The "Grandma Bandit" had lost no time. A passing car splashed slush over her oxfords and she made a swipe at the offending vehicle with her walking stick. I turned away from the window unable to witness any more raw aggression.

It grew later, darkness closed in and I realized with another shudder (not unlike the first) that I would soon have to leave the relative security of the building. I would have to venture out into the unpatrolled streets where chaos reigned unchecked.

A sobering thought it was. I couldn't very well take my table leg with me. I would probably be mistaken for a vandal and set upon and thoroughly pummelled by the hastily-formed people's militia.

So I would have to venture out under shot and shell with no protection. I tried to recall that neat judo trick in which the hero kicks the assailant in the knee and runs like heck. But under stress I couldn't remember if it was the right knee or the left.

At last the time came. Members of the staff were moving out in groups for mutual protection. I decided to go out alone for, when law and order are suspended, whom can you really trust?

I edged out the door. The edging bit was necessary because I had pushed a yardstick out into the shoulders of my jacket. I figured that would make them think twice.

The violence and looting were not immediately evident. As I moved up the street toward my conveyance I practiced the judo kick on two parking meters along the way.

This had an immediate effect. Two passers-by looked at me askance and gave me a wide berth and were obviously not ready to tangle. Two hoodlums they were, cleverly disguised as women shoppers.

I kept to the middle of the sidewalk under the street lights and avoided the dark alleyways, and put on a brisker step as I neared my horseless carriage.

Suddenly I saw three figures approaching. My heart gave a jolt. Ominous indeed. The one in the middle was wearing a maxi-coat, the two others were clad in mini-skirts.

The colour drained from me. I could see it staring me in the face. There I was with nothing with which to defend my virtue. Was I now to meet a fate worse than death in the lawless streets of St. John's?

For what, (if you objectively consider the package), has protected me all those years from the assaults of sex-crazed females if it is not the full weight and majesty of British law? The threat of the police, court and a jail sentence makes them think twice, that's what.

Now, fear froze me in my tracks. There was not a policeman in sight. As they came abreast I prepared for the pounce. I could do no more than offer up a silent prayer.

Nearer they came until I could see that the right nostril of the one in the maxi-coat was flaring slightly.

They passed on by!

My knees were weak, my palms were perspiring and I couldn't believe it.

Dumbfounded, I turned around and walked back past them. Still no reaction. Needless to say, I was severely shaken when I finally made it to my auto and locked the door behind me.

It is satisfying, in some ways, to see how well the general citizenry is holding the line in the face of a police strike.

In other ways, it's rather disappointing.

Just a Punt and a Jigger

In the light of present events some persons have been thinking, half-whimsically, that if things get too bad they can always go back and live the way we used to.

Impossible! No way! Even persons in the outharbours these days would be left just as helpless and floundering as town folk if the bottom dropped out.

"We could get along somehow, just like the old days," say some persons dreamily. "We wouldn't have to buy anything except tea, sugar, flour and a bit of tobacco."

No, there has been too much water under the bridge since then.

The subsistence fishing and farming bit is too impractical these days except for capricious well-to-do retirees or romantically-minded urban youths – and the latter panic at first snowfall anyway.

What a busy fall you would have ahead of you.

Although the means and "lifestyle" of outharbour people twenty or thirty years ago looked simple enough on the surface of it, this was certainly not the case.

Three or four lifetimes were needed to gather together those weathered cottages, stores, boats and fences which tourists think are so quaint.

The same amount of time was needed to acquire the knowledge

and skill as well as to cultivate both the personal and community family so necessary to live like that.

Suppose you've decided, despite warnings, to go right back to scratch, anyway.

Where's your horse?

First things first, and a pony is definitely your basic requirement.

You'll never plow up enough land to feed a family without a horse. Without a horse and boxcart it would take too much time to haul enough caplin, manure and kelp to fertilize it.

A tractor is too big, too expensive and too clumsy to turn in these small rocky gardens. And a roto-tiller, while suitable for plowing, is no good to haul your firewood out in the winter.

So you get a pony, tackle, cart and slide. How much hay have you got in the barn to feed it over the winter, and how much oats did you grow this summer to help the hay along?

You'll notice that just about every outharbour house has now got one of these fuel-oil tanks stuck up on stilts by the end of it. The oil tank replaced the coal shed which replaced the woodpile. If you're really going to do it from scratch you'll have to heat and cook with wood because you know what a ton or coal or a tankful of oil costs these days.

What it boils down to is that you'd better have enough cash in your pocket right now to buy a little premises around the bay, enough to outfit yourself with all manner of gear for next year's work, and enough to keep you and yours alive over the winter.

You can build a root cellar out back this fall, and plow up some ground for next spring, but where are you going to get the spuds to put in your cellar this winter?

How many of your lambs do you expect to kill this fall, and is it one pig or two? Is the cow still milking; can your wife card wool and knit; can you shoot a caribou or partridge?

Are your crocks of jam out in the cellar gone bad and are your barrels of herring headed up well?

Do you know the best place to send your youngsters after school to catch a meal of trout, and do they know where to find cocks-and-hens and mussels at low tide?

Will the goose be fat enough at Christmas?

If you are still entertaining notions of "going back to the country" you are a hard person to convince.

Okay, say you're going to get your feet wet gradually and not buckle down to brass tacks all at once.

You think you could get along on, say, quarter the money you're making now? Well, that's still a few thousand a year. I imagine the missus would perish without a telephone and electricity, and would rather bite the dust than let go her washer. So where's even this few thousand a year going to come from.

Are you going to make toy dories and mussel-shell ashtrays for the tourists, get a L.I.P. grant to do research on square blueberries, or heave yourself on long term assistance with a bad back?

Oh, you're goin' fishin' like your daddy fished before, are you?

Nothing big like a longliner. Just a punt and a jigger. A few lobster pots and a salmon net.

Oh, my poor man! Have you ever got another think coming. That sort of fishing is more complicated, more demanding of skill, experience, ability, lore and luck than putting together atomic bombs in a snowstorm in the dark.

These so-called "poor humble fishermen" had to have more knowledge tucked away in their weather-beaten skulls than a jet pilot has.

Nope, this inshore fishing racket is an exquisite art and no good for the likes of you or me to think we could master it in half a lifetime.

There has been too much water under the bridge since then.

Hints on the Rearage of Youngsters

I expect there will be some uncharitable persons who will say, "Oh, pooh. What does he know about the rearage of youngsters? I would as leave waste my time listening to Premier F. Duff Moores tell me how to run a country!"

There is nothing for it but to cast the aspersion back in their teeth.

Suffice it for me to say in defence that there's manys the good pediatrician as can tell you a thing or two about youngster rearage without ever having had one himself!

Of course, their little innards are best left in the hands of the medical fraternity and I make no pretensions in this sphere of rearing them.

I will confine myself to the practical side of rearage and merely offer the fruits of my observation of other people's little perishers over the course of many years.

There is, for example, the matter of keeping the average youngster vertical.

This strikes me as being a pressing problem and one which has received all too little attention over the years from such experts in the field of rearage as myself.

A notable feature of youngsters is that they are always falling down. They are exceedingly stunned in this regard as, indeed, in all others.

Your average infant will fall down as many as twenty or thirty times in the course of twenty-four hours. It is a distressing fact. The problem is of special magnitude on Sunday mornings when Daddy has a head from Saturday night, since some fallage gives rise to bawlage, loud and strong.

Here, we must correct ourself. For there are two sorts of infant fallage – the accidental noisy sort and the deliberate sort which is not injurious to household tranquility at all.

First, we shall deal with the deliberate kind.

Youngsters are, as has already been pointed out, exceedingly stunned. You might search the globe over and find nothing to equal them in stunnedness unless, perhaps, you stumble across the ranks of the Newfoundland government.

Hence, you get your youngster who has been toddling around the kitchen for a while in his diapers and in a more or less vertical position.

Presently, he becomes bored with this ambulatory exercise and wishes to become horizontal again on the floor, there to chew, probably, on some filthy old matchbox, et cetera, which he has found.

How to get from the vertical to the horizontal is a problem to which the infant noggin is not capable of finding a sensible solution.

A queer look comes over his little face. His eyes grow rounder and he gazes off into the distance. A slight blush suffuses his little cheeks.

In point of fact, he looks like an elderly matron who has just been goosed on the public streets or else a Cabinet Minister who has just been asked a sticky question during Supplementary Supply.

Slowly, he starts to fall backwards! Being bow-legged on top of being stunned he has fortunately not got far to fall. In the matter of a few seconds he had landed on the floor on his posterior with a considerable thump, from which position he rolls over unto his stomach.

He will do this time and time again in the course of an average day. Mercifully, this does not seem to hurt him and no screeching and bawling is entailed.

Poor foolish people will say, still, that there is no God!

I put it to you: Every school boy knows that in the old days of breast feedings it was damn nigh essential that little infants come into the world with no teeth.

But in modern times with the plastic nursebottle and the rubber nipple having supplanted all that, why are they still being popped along equipped with only the bare gums?

Ah, ha! Who else but a Higher Power would have taken into consideration that with teeth they would bite off their little tongues twenty times a day when they plopped themselves down on their backsides like that!

St. Augustine, if still living today, would have pointed out the self-same thing.

Next, we come to the other sort of youngster fallage, the so-called accidental noisy kind.

If noise pollution means anything at all to us (particularly on Sunday mornings) it is to this problem that we must apply ourselves.

At the risk of stressing the point overmuch, the minuscule capacity of the infant brain is here again the main cause.

It is only when he applies the full and undivided extent of his mental faculties to such a simple thing as toddling about the house that he can stay upright – and then only precariously.

Once his little mind starts to wander from the task at hand, once his attention is diverted away from toddling by some such thing as the cat's tail twitching, he completely forgets about his legs down there.

We all know what happens next. Down he falls and up she goes

In this sort of accidental fallage, he will usually pitch forward and cause himself some measure of temporary discomfort.

It is a shocking thing to observe and hear. His whole head dissolves into a little pink ball of soggy latex, and fearsome wails belying the size of their producer rattle the very window panes.

At this stage of the game, when we can put a man on the moon it is nothing short of astounding that we have not yet conquered this one main source of disquietude in the household.

When means have been struck upon to keep great ocean liners on an even keel in the midst of sixty-knot gales, is it not surprising that the world knows of no device by which to keep a twenty-pound infant upright on the kitchen floor?

What the answer is, I confess I do not know.

I must ask my mother about it next time I see her.

Little Blacks and Little Whites

There were, at last count, 736 different crises hanging over the world with imminent starvation being right up there among the top ten.

Supposing it is summer when the crunch comes, and supposing you are lucky enough not to be in that part of Newfoundland known as St. John's, you may – by emulating the Outharbour Juvenile's scavenging habits – gain one last afternoon in the world.

But only one, mind you, for although a good afternoon's scavenger, the Outharbour Juvenile always arrived back home with a good appetite for supper. In your case, of course, there'll be no supper there.

The little blackberry is your first source of sustenance. Found in July on the cliff-tops when the breeze is warm and the piercing cry of the sterin rises above the sparkling roar on the beach below.

What do they look like? How do you find them? How will you know them?

They're small as a pearl and black as the devil's Sunday shirt and you can hardly see them while standing, but if you get down on your knees you'll see them in hundreds and handfuls.

Since this is your last provender no doubt you will eat as much as you can and no doubt you will shuffle off your mortal coil due to starvation complicated by what is decorously termed "the summer complaint."

Too many blackberries have this effect on the digestion.

Your best bet of all might be to go off in the road and walk along until you get thirsty and come to a small brook. Your guts may jolly well be grumbling by this time, but, by cracky, here is a proper little snack for you.

Little white berries like emmet's eggs on string behind a rock by the brook. Hardly nothing at all to them except the taste, which is ten times better than peppermint knobs. You can even eat the little small leaves.

This is what is called maidenhair tea berries. They are not very substantial, even as gob-stoppers, but enough to scrape another afternoon on.

As luck might have it, world starvation may hit just on the afternoon of a low tide. In that case you're better off than the Outharbour Juvenile because you can go out on the rocks and get some mussels without getting a lacing for getting your feet wet when you get home.

Low as the tide may be, the very best mussels are always out just beyond the tops of your rubbers. It is nature's plan for selling more Vick's VapoRub...because the water is cold enough to make sharp pains shoot up through you; but you haven't got to mind that.

Once you have got your mussels the next thing you have to do is go out and get some more. It is a very poor run thing to stop getting mussels just because it looks like you've got enough. What looks like enough in the first instance won't be enough when they're all eaten and your stockings are warm if not dry in front of the fire. Getting your feet wet while wearing dry stockings is nothing at all, but getting your feet wet again while wearing warm wet stockings is something hellish.

So get enough in the first beginning. Light in your fire with a bit of wood on the beach that the fuel crisis overlooked, and sit there warm and hungry until it burns down a bit. No sense or reason to getting your mussels all full of flankers and soot. Then you put them on there until they open up, and then burn your fingers hooking them out.

Having thus won your final afternoon you will then starve to death when the sun goes down, with the nicest smell of wood smoke in the world on your clothes.

In High Places

Have you ever wondered what goes on in high places?

How would you like even a brief glimpse into the eighth floor of Conglomeration Building? To see first hand the germination of mighty works; to observe for a moment the interchange of lofty thoughts and great ideas; to stand at the elbows of the giants who direct Newfoundland's destiny?

A group of men, thin on top, large around the middle, sit around a huge table and, if you didn't know better, you'd say by the looks on their faces they were all extremely scared but had no place to run. Not so. It is neither desperation nor indigestion that causes them to look pasty – but the affairs of state weighing heavily on them.

The Skipper is speaking and their ears must not only be cocked but appear to be cocked. This accounts for the peculiar way they are sitting, and the rather unnatural angles at which they have inclined their necks. Now and then one of them may risk uncocking for a moment to study his fingernails – but only for a moment.

"I've seen them all, you know. The greats and the near-greats and the would-be greats. The great Sir Winston Churchill once said to me ...I forget just what it was now. The great Richard Nixon once gave me a big bear hug, and gentlemen, don't you forget it. How many of you have ever been given a big bear hug by the great Richard Nixon? Five? Four? Three? Two? One? I see. I see.

"The great, the very great, Eleanor Roosevelt once squeezed my elbow and said to me, 'Mr. Premier,' she said, 'isn't it great to be great like us?' 'Yes,' I said. 'Yes, it is.' I'm next to the Queen, you know. There's me and then there's Her Majesty.

"When was that? When was it that the great...? It was...wait, it's coming...It was at the opening of the great University that we have caused to be builded here. What year was that? What year is this? What? What?

"Snap, snap. Yes, you. I'm snapping my fingers at you. Eberhardt! Here, boy! Heel! Get that letter from my office. What letter? What letter? The one signed by my very good friend Richard Nixon himself, that's what letter. Snap, snap. Flooosh! Eberhardt! Go, go. Snap, snap.

"Mr. Jackdaw! Stop it! Stop it this instant! Is that any way for a minister of the crown to behave? Snap, snap. Dr. Jellyroll? Can you dance the polka? Dance, dance. Snap, snap. Sit down, sit down. That's me. Quiet! Quiet! That's me talking, you know. I'll turn it up and let you hear it. That's me on the radio.

"At the Lord Mayor's banquet there I was, lords to the right of me, lords to the left of me, dukes in front of me, dukes behind me.... Eberhardt! Snap, snap. Taste this sherry. They're out to get me, you know. They're all out to get me.

"We need a great new development for Passmaquodik Proper. What do you suggest? Quick, quick, quick! I don't keep dogs and bark myself. I want it and I want it now! A great new.... Quiet! Quiet! Snap, snap. That's me on again. That's me talking on the radio. You listen while I get the phone.

"Hello. Snap, snap. Quiet! Hello, John. Yes, John. I see, John. Right away, John. Yes, as fast as I can, John. No, I won't, John. Yes, I will, John. Don't worry about a thing, John. I'll be right there, John. Yes, John. No, John. Good-bye, John.

"Gentlemen, I go now to Panama to hold talks, vital talks, with the President of Panama. Sit there till I get back. Snap, snap."

Sliced for Your Convenience

I see they're even chopping bologna up into pound lots and wrapping it in plastic.

This must be a deuced inconvenience to the customer. Having served some time behind the counter myself, I know that the customer was rather fond of custom-cut bologna.

"Give us two thick slices, please, and three thinnish ones," was a common request. Or, "Cut them a bit thicker than you did last time and all the same size...or the youngsters'll fight."

When they had people staying with them you didn't have to ask as they always ordered a slice or two extra. Often as not, the younger customer ordered a slice at a time for consumption on the premises as a snack.

Pre-sliced bologna may be all very well but if it happens to be a bit rancid you'll end up with four or five slices green around the edges instead of just the first one off the loaf.

Just about everything comes tucked up in individual packages these days.

Though not so old as all that, I can recall when people made sure they got the tissue paper wrappings along with their oranges as proper toilet paper had not yet come on the market.

Getting molasses from the puncheon was a delicate job indeed.

The customers brought along their molasses cans and the trick was to ease out the spigot while holding the measure under it and at the same time loosening the top bung to allow vent.

Every now and then, due to some miscalculation, you'd get a shot of molasses up the sleeve and there are few more miserable experiences in the retail trade than being wet with molasses to the elbow.

Drawing off kerosene oil in cold temperatures was almost as bad. Colder than the coldest ice water it was, and if you splashed some on your hands you'd get these darting pains right to the top of your head.

Tea came in large chests and had to be measured out with a little scoop. Peas and beans arrived in burlap bags which were dumped out with a great roar and a cloud of dust into tin bins.

Cheese was a large wheel and cutting off a pound of it took great exercise, and considerable calculation was needed to get the right heft the first time and not have to hack off little bits to make up weight.

Biscuits of numerous sorts came in large wooden boxes and so did dried apricots, apples, peaches and prunes.

All had to be weighed out to individual order in paper bags, and if the customer thought a pound didn't look like enough he had only to say, "Oh, chuck in another handful or so."

Beef wasn't so bad (except for jamming your arms down in the frigid pickle and realizing you had a few hangnails you hadn't noticed), but getting out the first couple of pieces of pork from a new barrel was always a tussle. The pork was stowed in so tightly there was nothing on which to get a hold and a newly opened barrel presented a real puzzle.

Bacon came in slabs and each rasher has to be sawed off by hand.

All the candy came either in cardboard boxes lined with waxed paper or in large bottles.

Apples arrived in wooden barrels in the fall and the fine smell of an apple barrel is, to my mind, three parts of an apple.

Even soft drinks first came in wooden barrels packed in straw and the bottles were of no particular size, brand or flavour...just a random selection of whatever the packers had available.

Nails, in their heavy burlap bags, were torture to gouge out by the handful and weigh. It was much like trying to strangle a porcupine. Sugar from its hundred-pound sack was a different matter.

But flour was always sold by the sack, never, until recent times, by the stone. At first there was no "bakers bread" and when it did arrive it was not "sliced for your convenience."

Lemon crystals, that favourite of children and grandmothers in the summer, came in a large crock and had to be measured out.

People brought their own shopping bags – commodious affairs made of heavy cloth attached to wooden handles.

There were none of those large paper bags seen today which always seem to rip at the worst time. And although there were some tins and bottles, there were certainly no plastic packages.

The chief advantage of having things in bulk was that the edibles such as bacon or cheese kept longer and fresher in those days before refrigeration and that the customer could order no more nor less than he wanted.

Now if you buy a package of cheese, not only is the pound of it wrapped up in tough plastic, but each thin and weakly slice inside is also individually wrapped.

I fancy that even the bulk tea was better and kept a flavour longer than tea does now scattered about in small packages where the air has a better chance to rob it.

True enough, if a barrel of apples or a bologna or a bottle of candy didn't get used up on schedule and commenced to rot or go bad or melt, there was a certain loss but that – in theory, at least – was the shopkeeper's rather than the customer's.

String and wrapping paper went out when the supermarkets and "pre-packaging" came in. But, for all that, by the time you get a few bags of groceries opened and consumed these days there seems to be more packages to it than there are edibles.

Most of the convenience of this system goes, I should think, to the storekeepers rather than the customers.

It is not nearly as much labour and, if you want only a pound and two slices of bologna nowadays you have to buy two pounds.

And do people really prefer it sliced so abominably thin? In my day behind the counter they'd think you were somehow trying to rob them.

East Meets West

We stood halfway up the slope at Marble Mountain and watched the toy cars creep back and forth the Humber Valley far below. On either side of this spectacular valley the first frosts of fall have tinged the vegetation. But at the bottom the fall colours are much brighter. The early frosts, you see, flow down the slopes and settle on the narrow river plain so that the trees blaze brightest near the base of these towering walls and flicker away to paler shades near the top.

Magical, fluorescent colours, almost unreal and artificial when the late afternoon sun strikes an isolated tree from behind. It glows as if by its own light against a background of dark and straight evergreens.

Each birch tree a shower of bright gold against a crisp blue autumn sky; each dogberry a glowing mass of delicate amber and orange lace; each mountain maple and wild cherry a fluttering cascade of scarlet and crimson.

The Humber Valley in mid-October is like a giant's flower garden. On dark days in spring or summer the soaring walls of the gorge are almost oppressive in their gloomy splendor. But in autumn, the lights are turned on and the brightest Christmas streets of large cities are dull by comparison.

Our east coast has nothing like it. To be sure, the low eastern woods are rich and mellow in the fall haze and the barrens are a burgundy when the frost touches the blueberry bush and the marshes are dull gold.

But it is very tame and pleasingly melancholy compared to the heady exuberance, the unearthly brilliance of the great glowing canyons of our west.

Three hundred and fifty years ago, St. John's must have looked a bit like Corner Brook does today.

We are told that when Humphrey Gilbert landed, the hills were clothed in thick forest and the shores of the clear sparkling harbour were like a garden where you might walk among the raspberries and wild roses.

Fires and the axe and the bulldozer and dynamite and asphalt and cement have long since reduced Signal Hill and the Southside to a picked skeleton.

But Corner Brook is still fresh and handsome. The approaches to it by land or sea are magnificent. Its site must be the most splendid of any town this side of the Rocky Mountains.

If you wanted to be really malicious toward old Sin John's, then Corner Brook provides plenty of ammunition.

Imagine, for instance, a page of pictures of Corner Brook side by side with a page of pictures of St. John's:

St. John's General Hospital with decaying sheds and rusting car wrecks in the foreground – Western Memorial Hospital overlooking Bowater Park and swans on the river.

Valley Road in Corner Brook with the homes sunk amid towering poplars and maples – a residential street in a new St. John's development with a grave-mound patch of grass in front and miserable little buggy whips with ten leaves apiece.

Corner Brook's West Street, swank for its size with the fountains in front of Holiday Inn and still more trees, put up against the wires and grime and bastardized shop-fronts of Water Street.

Even the government building at Corner Brook is handsome and in keeping with its setting compared to that garish monstrosity hunkered down in the teeth of a perpetual gale behind St. John's.

On every hand there are cruel comparisons. Glynmill Inn, a fake Tudor hotel set in a mid-town park at Corner Brook, and that slab of tired bricks facing a suicidal jumble of intersections at Fort William in St. John's.

Kenmount Road versus Shellbird Island. Topsail Highway against the Long Range Mountains. Waterford River and the Humber. The Southside and Summerside.

Among all the scenic perfection of Corner Brook there is one large blemish, and that is, of course, the mill itself, located directly at the centre on the waterfront.

It was the mill that created Corner Brook but on certain days when the wind is the right way a sulphurous stench hangs over the town. The fumes have burned a nearby hill face down to bare rock – a small sample of St. John's as it is after three-and-a-half centuries.

There are other little jarring notes, but in all, Corner Brook and the Bay of Islands is stunningly fair. It must be one of the happiest marriages between man and nature anywhere. An Easterner is bedazzled by the sudden change from the squalid captivity and grimy alleys of Bagdad-Upon-Cesspool to the limitless freedom and stark beauty of our Western City.

This is not to indicate a hatred of the poor, poor people of Sin John's. Far from it.

It is rather an expression of pity for all the poor, good people of this Eastern Disaster who are trapped in it and who languish in helplessness as they see their community being mangled and chopped up and turned into an unlovely, unlivable hell-hole.

Nowhere does the difference between the squalor (both old and new) of Sin John's, and the freshness of the rest of the Country strike the escaped convict so hard as when he makes it as far as our West Coast.

And at no time of the year does the contrast between nature trampled into the muck and nature in glory become so apparent as during the month of October.

Then, of all seasons, our western hills blaze with a splendour that sucks the spirit of the beholder up into the blue air and leaves the body as light as a little dicky bird.

Outharbour Youth's Guide to
Sin John's

Some helpful hints and pointers for the outharbour youth planning his first visit to suave, swinging, sophisticated Sin John's.

They are being presented here in hope of saving many youthful Baymen from the pitfalls and tight spots that bestrew the boulevards and avenues of the glittering Capital.

Since they drove the people off New Gower Street to make room for a pile of concrete fish boxes which they call the new City Hall, the heart of St. John's is now Brazil Square and Water Street West.

You will find the boarding houses on Brazil Square a lot dearer than they used to be, so bring plenty of money. This is because they have knocked off putting four boarders in one bed. The modern custom of one customer to one bed is not only unsociable, it drives up their heating bills and the extra expense is passed on to you.

Nevertheless, you are lucky to be staying right in the heart of Sin John's. Brazil Square might not be all of Sin John's but there's not much else to see further up except a lot of small houses all crammed together and spread out in all directions.

Such interesting sights as the Gaol, the Lunatic Asylum and the Conglomeration Building are miles apart since somebody lacked the good sense to put them all under one roof.

One of the first things you will want to do is get a mug-up on stuff that you are not used to at home. Woolworth's is not a bad spot for this, although you had better ask for two hot turkey sandwiches if you don't want to be gutfoundered before supper. And get one of those banana splits, as they call them.

You can't buy a decent cup of tea anywhere in Sin John's so don't waste your money on it. In any case, there is no place to make a drop of water unless you go back to your boarding house. If you dart into an alley you will be chastized. This might seem a curious setup until you realize that all the livyers go around with hot water bottles strapped to their legs.

But you are safe enough in the taverns in that regard. They have what they call "washrooms" for the purpose.

Aside from the Belmont and the Porthole and perhaps a few more, all the taverns in Sin John's will get you down in the dumps as soon as you face in around the door. They are all fancy places and the liquor is dear in them, but you never saw such a gloomy looking crowd in your life. They are all having a "good time".

At the Belmont, you might see certain chaps with chin whiskers and scruffy clothes looking at you. They are what they call sociologists and anthropologists and what not from the university. They are "studying" you, which is the height of ignorance, but never mind.

If one talks to you, then you can get a rise out of him by telling him that you killed your father with an axe when you were fourteen, and that you were reared on codsheads and screech. That will make him overjoyed.

Don't venture to speak to anyone you see on the street. This used to be done, but not any more. They will think you are going to take their money purses or something and will call the constables.

They seem a little on the touchy side and quick to get out of sorts. It is because they never had the advantages you had while being reared up. All hands are stogged together on top of each other in Sin John's, and this gives them bad nerves. Apart from that they are very good sorts.

If you are out for a bit of sport, there is none in St. John's, I'm afraid. You will see many young maids with their skirts up across their quarters and their faces done up who waggle their backsides, but they will turn out to be twelve-year-old schoolgirls and not to be tampered with. Perhaps you know some young maid from home who is in service in St. John's or going to school. However, she will cut you every time. There is nothing so stuck up as a Baygirl in Sin John's...or the other way around.

So it is best to forget your bit of sport and think pure thoughts like your mother told you.

Don't take any nonsense from motor cars or you will be pegged for a Bayman right away. Walk scow-ways across the street as slow as you can and dare them to hit you. Shake your fist at them and curse them up in heaps.

If you happen to be in company with a chap who is driving a motor car, this can be great fun also. Speed up when you see people crossing the street and see how handy you can come to their quarters and splash them with slush whenever possible.

After another hot turkey sandwich or two, it will be time to take the bus home. If you found Sin John's interesting, but got a few unkind cuts from the livyers and what not, think on what you learned in Sunday School:

"All things bright and beautiful, all creatures great and small; all things wise and wonderful, the Lord God made them all."

And if you are thinking of going to Toronto some day looking for something to do, remember that Toronto is much like Sin John's except that there's a damn sight more of it.

Strange Paradise

On the eve of momentous occasions such as the start of National Pickle Week, the official opening of great new orange juice factories, and Budget Day, it is my custom to go down to the public streets and feel the public pulse.

When seeking to find which way the wind blows you can do a lot worse than eavesdrop on the common man. Since the next day would bring us the Budget Speech, I had no doubt that the marketplace would be buzzing with talk of little else.

I seated myself at random in a city restaurant, cocked one ear, and prepared to take whatever the good Lord sent me. I find this method to be more hygenic than messing around in a bunch of goat entrails.

At the adjacent table sat two citizens who were clearly of voting age and I tuned in on their conversation:

"...one awful gash, my dear. She was cut from here right down to here and then scow-ways over across to here. She told me...now I'm only speakin' after her, mind you...that she had forty-three stitches and they the biggest kind."

"Well!!"

"Oh, yes, my dear. You'd hardly know her at all to look at her. She fell right away and she always used to be so jolly. She told me that she was down now to, I think it was, 163 pounds and every stitch she got is away too big for her. Before that, you know, she was under three doctors in two months, so Mildred tells me, and back and forth two and three times a week."

"My!"

"Yes, and pills, my dear. You talk about pills. Two big orange-colour ones and three brown and yalla tablets four times a day. Cost a fortune if she wasn't under the department. Before they opened her up, you know, they only had intentions of taking half of it out.

"But when they got her open, she said, they thought it was just as well to make the job of it. 'Yes, my dear,' I told her, 'and so it was, too. You'll have comfort now,' I said, 'and that's something you never had before.'

"I know that's the way I found it when I had mine. She didn't mind it at all. Oh, no. The worst thing she minded, she said, was the clotherfarm. She thought she might be cursin' and swearin' when she was comin' out of it."

"You talk about!"

"Didn't mind it one bit, my dear. So good as a holiday, she says. Didn't care if they chopped it all out and tacked it up on the wall right in front of her eyes. Her very words, my dear. I had to laugh because I couldn't help it."

By this time I was getting qualmish but I considered it nothing less than my duty to keep listening until the conversation got around, as surely it must, to Budget Day. Just then the waitress came along and after I had placed my order for the Monday special, stewed cockroach with veg. and chips, the conversation had indeed taken another turn:

"...stood in line from a half past eight o'clock in the morning until they opened the doors at half past nine. I turned around to this big stocky one behind me and I says, 'Look a'here, missus. You sticks me in the back one more time with that umbrella you got there and you're goin' to get one awful root.' My very words.

"'Well,' she says, so bold as brass, she says, 'You keep your quarters to yourself and you won't get stuck in the back with neither umbrella.'"

"Well!"

"Oh, yes, my dear. I can tell you we would of had it out hot and warm right then and there, because I was just the one to give her so good as she send, if they hadn't opened the doors. You had to watch your step then. You knows what 'tis like."

"Yes, my dear, and indeed I do know what 'tis like."

"They never had nothin' extra. I had up a pair of them 93 cent panty hose on the five-minute super special and I had half a mind to have 'em but this other streel, she grabbed hold of one leg and we took 'em in two at the fork. Oh, me poor feet. Three hours, my dear I didn't think I'd be able to make it so far as the bus stop."

"Well! Never worth it, is it?"

"No, my dear, never worth it. I see there's one at the Mall on Friday and I'm on two minds about goin', I can tell you that. I dare say I might, though, if I can see my way clear."

"How is your sister-in-law now?"

"Well, my dear, she's up one day and down the next. That's about the size of it. She eats like the horse but she don't seem to pick up at all.

"She'll get up and watch "As the World Turns" and then she might watch "Edge of Night" if she feels up to it and then she might swing the dust rag around for five minutes and then she'll have someting to eat and take another nap. And that's her day, apart from Bingo nights.

"I told her, 'My dear,' I said, 'you'll have to take yourself in hands and try and make the effort. Why don't you come along in company with me tomorrow morning,' I said, 'downtown to the Bankrupt Bonanza.' I said. 'It might do you the world of good.'

"Well, she said she might and she mightn't, all according to whether she feeled up to it, she said, but she didn't have the energy for nothin', she said. I pities her, honest to God, I do. There in that big house all day long with nothing to do except eat and sleep and watch a bit of television. She's really lettin' herself go now, that's what I think of it and that's the God's truth.

"You won't believe what she told me the other day. I wouldn't want this to get around for the world but she told me the other day – and this is true as I'm sitting here – she said there was days, she said, when she didn't even have the strength, she said, to ring up Phone Phorum! Now! What do you think of that and she still a young woman."

"Tut, tut, tut."

"Yes, my dear, and that's what I says about it too, I talks to her and I talks to her but it don't seem to do much good. Certainly, you don't like to be all the time buttin in. I know I don't. I pities poor Waynwright more than I pities anyone else. Well, that was a lovely drop of tea. Oh. I s'pose we won't see "Strange Paradise" tomorrow."

"Oh, and how is that my dear?"

"That old Budget as they calls it, my dear. I s'pose that'll be blastin' away all day tomorrow. My, I hardly sees the sense of havin' a television set at all these days."

"Yes, and that's for sure. They fools it up all the time. The last time it was on from Consideration Building I watched it for a little while but they'd only show Mr. Smallwood on there now and again. So I said what's the good of it, and I turned it off altogether. Well, I s'pose we must go."

Perhaps there's such a thing - when you go out into the market place seeking the reactions of the common man - as chancing upon a sample that is too damn common.

Anyway, we can all take heart in the knowledge that the vote now extends to everyone who's of age except jailbirds, lunatics and royalty.

In the Mice

Some people might claim that being in the mice is a refreshing change from the rats but I would have my doubts.

Mice is what I'm in at the current time and it is no picnic I can assure you.

Since moving to my present domicile a few years ago, I have caught the glimpse of only one cat in the neighbourhood. And a glimpse it was. She was travelling like a streak of spit through a tin whistle in the general direction of Kelligrews with about one inch of tail stuck straight in the air.

Dogs, you see. Nearly all the livyers keep one or two. Some are about the heft of a block of butter and others can step over a picket fence without grazing their gut.

A cat would have about as much chance out here as a one-eyed caplin in a school of sharks.

Consequently, with the cats away the mice will play...as the old saying goes. Well and good in the summer when they're content to play ring-around-the-rosie out of doors. But at the first touch of frost they make a mad scramble for the house.

And with not so much as a crackie around the premises it seems that about three parts of the little flamers on this shore prefer to shack out the winter in the ceiling at Chez Guy.

Perhaps you have not had the experience of a mouse invasion and think it cannot be all that hard on the nerves.

You have got another think coming. Many more nights of this and they'll catch me sending letter bombs to Mickey Mouse. Much more of this and I expect the mere sight of a pair of ear muffs will turn me homicidal.

Why, on the Blessed Sabbath just past when I would normally be deep in contemplation and meditation perusing Scriptures, I was turning laps around the house waving a kitchen chair over my head.

Driven to a frenzied blood-lust directly contrary to my nature, I came within a hair's breath of doing myself in for good on Saturday night past as we shall see.

As you might know, the ravenous little brutes, once safely inside out of autumn's chilling blast, make directly for the loft. Once there, they skitter about in the most annoying and insulting fashion and conduct God-knows-what sort of obscene orgies up there among the fiberglas insulation.

On Saturday night past they were especially hard at it, clumping about and squealing drunkenly in what can only have been the most disgustingly depraved binge since Nero cashed in his chips.

Talk about the inconvenience of apartment living. At least if the party upstairs gets too rough you can always call the cops. But have you phoned the constabulary lately to complain about obstreperous mice?

No, you would be thought less of and spoken of quite rudely by the lads at the station. So you are entirely on your own and at the mercy of these bewhiskered, nihilistic hoodlums.

I stood the little bleeders as long as I could. But the longer you sit there with that "scrotch, scrotch, squeek, squeek, scamper, scamper" being dinned into your ears, the more tense you get.

They're up there, you know, chewing the stuffings out of your insulation and driving your winter's heating cost through the end of the thermometer.

In a sudden spate of fury, I sprang from my chair and pitched a copy of Emerson's *Society and Solitude* full force at the ceiling, which volume rebounded and struck me just above the right eye.

This set them off altogether and I knew that now it was going to be total war.

In times of stress I find the sensibilities heightened, the reflexes even more lively than usual, the mind a steel trap with frost on it.

It was to the traps I sprang having remembered on the instant these deadly weapons in the kitchen cupboards where they had reposed since last year's autumnal conflicts ended in a draw.

Alongside the traps, cruel little snappers crafted in Germany, was a leftover box of terrible poison plastered fore and aft with dire warnings and even worse antidotes.

I was going to give them both barrels. Not that I have much faith in the poison. When I climb up the stepladder and hoist the hatch to lodge the stuff on the rafters for them they just about knock me down in the rush to get at it.

All it does, I'm sure, is make them twice as fat, twice as frolicsome, and twice as ignorant and foul-mouthed.

But, anyway, I was prepared to go along with chemical warfare again and thought it would at least lure them along close enough for the traps to get a snap at them.

A bit of cheese in each of three traps cocked and primed to a quivering hair trigger, and in the other hand the opened box of Agatha Christie's best oatmeal.

"Here's the medicine for you hedonistic Mongol hordes!" I announced loudly as I mounted the stepladder in the closet towards the hatch to the loft. "Prepare to meet Walt Disney!"

Actually, I didn't think shouting at them would do much good except to back them away from the trap door a bit to hover in the corners with their frightful red eyes shooting sparks of menace at me.

As near as I can make out it was an old sneaker boot that did it. One foot of the stepladder, you see, had been rested in the heat of the moment on an old sneaker boot rather than on the solid floor.

It gave way the instant I had placed my three engines of death in a row on the rafters, and was about to set down the fatal package of Acme Jim Dandy Mouse-Tox alongside them.

In a frantic grab to save myself I thrust several fingers of one hand into the cheesy grog bits and in the ensuing agony grabbed the box of strychnine salad with the other.

The rapid descent to the floor of the closet was accomplished with only minor damage, but I got the whole shower of Mouse-Tox in the face and eyes and up the nasal passages.

I must say that at this point reason more or less left me. If this is the way I'm down on the books to go, I'd just as soon have the privilege of picking my own poison.

Though in stark terror I seemed to recall that as good an antidote as any in these cases is cold water, and I made a lunge for the convenience.

Panic had so befuddled me that I unscrewed both bathtub and basin faucets at once and got only the merest dribble from each – not recalling that since my water trouble of last year my pressure is much below what it should be.

Uncharitable persons would, I suppose, like to hear that I then followed the obvious course and dived head and ears into the crapper.

Ah, no. They shall not have their satisfaction. I plunged out the back door where a brisk downpour was in progress and stood under the eaves until every particle of the noxious substance was washed away.

The next day when relating these trails and tribulations to an – as I thought – sympathetic colleague, he looked at me oddly and said: "Chee! You'd better get a woman out there as quick as you can!"

What is the world has that got to do with it?

Is the poor fellow balanced?

I'd almost suspect he's been in the mice even longer than I have!

Getting the Outharbour Juvenile Rigged For Winter Months

The secret of draught-free juvenile winter wear is a good set of drawers. Encased from chin to ankle in such a garment he was ready for any climatic extreme. This homemade body stocking was constructed of wool straight from the back of the sheep with some of the twigs left in it.

In a proper suit of home-knit drawers he could have walked to the North Pole and back clad in nothing else. However, this was only the foundation. A well-made drawer is faced down the front with strips of flour sacking and the trap door around the back neatly faced in like manner.

If it looked to be an especially sharp winter, a chest protector was added which is to say, several doubles of heavy flannel were affixed inside the drawer against the bosom so that the juvenile respiratory system was doubly protected. There is no snugger garment.

Home-knit drawers had only one defect of manufacture. After several years of washings they were affected by a complaint known as fork droop. The garment tended to stretch and sag over the years so that the crotch fell to about the knees. Apart from causing a slight impediment in the juvenile's gait, this was nothing serious.

Then came hose. The inner pair of stockings, also home-knit, were thigh length and kept in place well above the fork droop line by a set of garters.

The second pair of stockings were knee-length and drawn on over the first. Lucky the lad with a bright red top to these outer stockings which flashed jauntily above the tops of his boots.

Vamps came next. Hand-knit from the self-same material, these socks came to just above the knobs of the ankles and were worn over the first two sets of hose.

Over the flannel chest protector and the woolen drawers went the outside shirt. Today's shirts are mere toys compared to the heft and thickness of those robust garments.

Then what is perhaps the piéce de rèsistance of the whole juvenile winter ensemble was drawn on. The set of briggs. Or "breeks" as they were called by some. These garments were forged from material of an inch thickness which had been woven from quarter inch manilla rope and guaranteed to "stand up."

It is hard to picture the effect caused by this piece of dry goods. They were reinforced at the knees with patches of the stoutest leather with slits in the legs which were snugly fitted against the juvenile calf by means of an arrangement of lacings.

They were supported upon the person from the shoulders by means of another piece of rubber wear...the braces, as they are called in the U.S., or suspenders, as they are known in Great Britain. Such an arrangement produced a curious phenomenon.

Since the garment was always purchased two sizes too large to allow for expansion of the occupant over the course of time, the breeks hung loosely. Whenever the juvenile broke into a brisk trot, the heavy breeks sagged up and down on the elastic suspenders.

Fitted out in breeks, the juvenile cut a considerable dash. He looked not unlike a veteran drummer boy from the Great War or a dwarf Mountie doing undercover work among criminal midgets. Thus, briggs.

More wool was then applied in the shape of a sweater which went over the flannel chest protector, the woollen drawers, the shirt and the braces. Whilst other wool garments tended to stretch in time, sweaters, for some reason, always shrunk.

Our attention is now directed to the juvenile foot. You may recall that it is encased in the long stocking, the knee stocking and the vamp. A pair of logans, described elsewhere, completed the picture.

Alas, it was never the author's privilege to own a pair of logans, the most dashing sort of footwear next to the long rubber. He had to make do with the gum boots, the same worm by the Present Sovereign and family when mucking about Balmoral on weekends.

Into each boot went a felt which is a hunk of material, purple in colour, constructed from the fur of the Australian rabbit and shaped like the sole of a foot. Felts insulated further and absorbed moisture. They were dried behind the stove at night.

In the days before parkas were popularized, the upper part of the torso was topped off by either an old suit jacket, handed down by some older relative, or a windbreaker.

Hand protection came in the form of mitts. If double-knit, one pair sufficed; if single, two pairs were worn. There are few things more unhandy than a new pair of mitts. The palms come to a point about six inches beyond the fingertips making a good purchase on a snowball impossible.

However, in about a month of wear a strange substantiation takes place in which the new mitt perfectly assumes the shape of the hand. Old mitts smell nice. They get turpentine on them and when drying under the kitchen stove release the scent of balsam fir so that there is no need for synthetic pine in a spray can.

So much for mitts. We are ready for the headgear. There is only one piece of goods equal to topping the fully dressed juvenile in proper fashion and that is the aviator cap.

This dashing leather helmet is designed after the self-same cap worn by the herioc Lindbergh on his solo crossing of the Atlantic Ocean. In fact, all outharbour juvenile winter wear was on an heroic model – from the Royal Northwest breeks to the Scandinavian forester logans to the Lindbergh headpiece, he cut no mean figure.

With the addition of a flannel scarf to chink any cracks in these coldweather garments thought which drifts might enter, the outharbour juvenile's winter regalia was complete.

He was set to face the raging blizzards and crackling frost and thy cloak of shimmering white spread at winter's sterm command. Blizzards! Lord save us, with the simple addition of an oxygen bottle he was ready for leisurely strolls upon the surface of the moon.

Out from daylight to dark and the worse it came the better with only two nostrils and one eye sticking out and the drifts building up as high as the houses and the wind ninety knots an hour and it getting darker and colder and the snow still coming down and in the white whirl you can't see a double-knit mitt in front of your face. What? We worry?

Central heating in the houses and schools and heated school busses have come along. But the juvenile, outharbour and in, must still wait out at least a few minutes at the bus stops and that in mini skirts or grey flannel trousers.

Either the winters are getting milder or the breed is getting still hardier.

A Dreadful Kind of Good

There was a particularly nasty accident, as I recall, on the railroad tracks or the telegraph line in which one poor man belonging to our place was killed.

An oldish man was passing the news along to another.

"Did you hear what happened to poor so-and-so this morning?"

"Yes, my dear man, I did so. 'Tis wonderful, wonderful! Wonderful altogether!"

Certain words did not mean the same thing in the Newfoundland speech then as they do now. And, of course, words were used differently from one place to another.

It was easier to spot what seemed to be peculiar words when spoken by people from other places than it was to recognize them in our own speech.

Because, naturally, we thought we were speaking the King's English better than the King did.

For instance, some chums who used to come up from Bell Island for the summer holidays through it quite amusing to hear the word "directly" used so often at Arnold's Cove.

"Directly" didn't mean, as the dictionary tells us, right away or at once either.

It means "in a little while" or "by and by" as in "You go on over.

I'll be along directly." "You 'bide right there now. I'll be back again directly."

Some pronounced the word "da-WRECK-ly", while among the linguistic mutants at the other end of the harbour it was "da-WRECK-ry".

We, in turn, were amused by the way the people from Mussel Harbour (later, Kingwell after Parson Kingwell) on Long Island used the word "dreadful".

Everything with them seemed to be dreadful. "I'm DREAD-ful fond of them polar bars," or " 'Tis a DREAD-ful nice day" or "The weather is a DREAD-ful kind of poor."

Things could also be a DREAD-ful kind of good.

Even three miles across the harbour at Bordeaux the inhabitants used certain phrases which could cause much merriment at Arnold's Cove.

Once, when the 'flu' was rampant, Great Uncle Tom Eddy rowed down to the cove and, of course, the first question was "And how is all your crowd, Uncle Tom?"

"Only poorly, men. Only poorly. Maggie is all knocked up and Triffie is knocked up and I'm knocked up meself."

In the progressive community of Arnold's Cove the phrase, used by Queen Victoria herself to indicate any complaint or illness, had already become a euphemism for pregnancy

We used to think that the people belonging to Tack's Beach "talked wonderful brogue-ish." To be sure, they were Protestants but they had such names as Best and Brown and the girls seemed remarkable to us, having come of age, for their generally dark hair, rosy pink cheeks and splendid – if I may say so – limbs.

And of course the people belonging to Southern Harbour also sounded "wonderful brogue-ish."

Wonderful, indeed. A pretty thing to listen to. Not so harsh, I fancy, as the St. John's brogue and it always reminded me, for some reason, of a little brook running down over the rocks.

The Southern Harbour people seemed to make much use of the phrase "but sure.." which they pronounced "bed shure.." as in, "Bed shure, there's no sense nor raisin to it these days, atall, atall."

Please to be assured there is nothing at all in this of making fun of people. Certainly not.

We didn't use the word "clever" to mean smart. But, on second thought, we did. Today, "clever" means much the same as "smart" but then neither meant the same as, say, being proficient in school or good at taking Acadias apart.

We would say, "My, what a clever baby," or "That's some clever set of oars you got there," meaning, in the first case, that the baby was healthy looking and, in the second instance, that the oars were well constructed.

"Cute" meant sort of sly or, in the case of animals, being remarkably intelligent.

Thus, "Oh, he's just so cute as the fox, sir," or "That dog, sir, is just so cute as the Christian."

On the other hand, "smart" meant in good health and brisk spirits – "How is your mother these days? Is she still smart?" "Yes, thank God. Smart as the top."

As youngsters, we didn't catch on to all the words right from the start.

For instance, us juvenile lads were puzzled one evening when we went along to pick up, let us say, our comrade Benedict for the usual walk in the road with the girls to see the train go by.

No, said his mother, Benny wasn't getting out of the house. Benny would have to be watched from now on and kept down more.

"How is that, Miz Guy, ma'am?"

"If 'tis any of your business atall" – for she, having come from another place, was wonderful brogue-ish – "he have entered into puggerty."

Good Lord! Was it catching? In a manner of speaking, it was. After much research and considerable embarrassment at a few dinner tables we found that sooner or later we would all enter into poor Benny's interesting state which was, as they say in the Boston States, puberty.

"Gross talk" didn't mean coarse language or swearing but that the speaker had a deep bass voice and could be heard afar off on a calm day.

One person from the cove, always noted for his gross voice, happened along at an awkward time some years ago.

A man from a community nearby had "gone away" and entered the clergy. Having made good in that line of business – he was a Canon or something – he now appeared in collar and ecclesiastical gaiters to renew old acquaintances.

He was down in a lobster factory talking to the boys when the man with the gross voice came in. They immediately started to play a little game which is played.

"Come here, Steve" - we'll call him - "see if you knows this man here."

The usual amused glances back and forth and the comical little wait to see how long it would take Steve to recognize the visitor and his astonishment at having done so.

There was about thirty seconds of silence while recognition sunk in. Then came the fearful roar: "KRISE, BILL, 'TIS NOT YOU IS IT?"

If good things appeared in large quantities the amount was described as "A wonderful sight" such as, "No mistake, there's a wonderful sight of fish out there. All big fish, too."

But if bad things turned up in large numbers it was "A shockin' sight" as, "There's a shockin' sight of sea dabs (jelly fish) out there today." Other things coming in shockin' sights to foul nets were, of course, dog fish and whore's eggs. You may know the latter as "sea urchins", ma'am.

I can mind (remember) a lot more of these words but sometimes I wish I had written them down fresh on the spot.

Because your memory starts to slide, I think, once you enter into puggerty.

An Unhealthy Trend

There's something indecent - for want of a better word - about this new and growing interest in politics on the part of the average Newfoundlander. There's something not...well, not Newfoundland about it.

It's time this new fad was nipped in the bud.

Politics should be left to the politicians. It's a full time job with them, they're paid well out of public funds. What inefficiency, confusion and duplication results when the general public tries to dabble in politics.

The traditional role of the general public in Newfoundland with regard to politics is being trampled under. Politics used to be a parlour game, a spectator sport, in which the man in the street discussed, grumbled and criticized from fall to spring but never dreamed of doing anything more than that about it.

There's an alarming trend of late for the amateurs - the general public - to become involved, to do something more than talk. We see large numbers of citizens actively involved even at the municipal level.

The depth of involvement on the part of the young, for instance, has already reached unseemly proportions. It is the sort of thing which must be discouraged if order and civil serenity are to be maintained.

It is nothing less than frightening to find that the average

Newfoundlander is actually concerned about the government of the province. Not only concerned, but anxious to do something about it.

Where this kind of outrageous insolence will lead we fear to speculate. There are people either elected or appointed to do that sort of thing for us.

Yet we find that students at the university, for example, are actually becoming interested in the government of Newfoundland and in the future course of the province! Gadzooks!

Are there not enough sock hops and panty raids and beer-drinking contests to keep them out of such mischief? Are not logarithms, Chaucer and the number of angels that can dance on the head of a pin enough to keep them occupied?

Events have reached a pretty pass indeed when we find that even unschooled persons of the middle and lower classes are seriously venturing opinions on politics and government.

This upstart meddling by amateurs is especially dangerous in these times when the situation of the province is rather critical, and urgent, not to mention chaotic. Is it not irresponsible to interfere with the officers on the bridge in time of storm?

Politics should be left to the politicians. It is a matter of absolutely no concern to the average citizen and not a fit topic for general discussion.

Let the population go about its business and leave government entirely in the capable and rightful hands of those who have been set in authority over us.

Splendour

Success to our sister, Labrador!

While the politicos scramble back and forth down here on the Island and insular tumults and alarums clog nearly every minute and inch of the "Newfoundland" press, let us give at least a passing thought to our great northern territory.

How many Newfoundlanders now living on the Island can, with a clear conscience, claim that Labrador is a part of their Country and belongs to them? To make such a claim and back it up with anything more than sheer gall, you need not have actually visited Labrador. It isn't necessary to have relatives or acquaintances living there, although many Island dwellers have.

But if you are going to jump up on a box once every six months and talk about "our" northern part called Labrador, you have at least got to show some evidence of good faith.

This means that you must have shown enough interest in Labrador to find out as much as you could about it and become informed on exactly what the heck there is on the other side of the Straits of Belle Isle.

The Newfoundland media will have to be forced by public pressure to pay more attention to Labrador. They won't do it freely because it isn't economical. There's not enough advertising up there; it costs too much to send reporters and photographers too far outside St. John's; they haven't got enough viewers and readers up north.

Here's irony for you. What is the chief text, sermon, epistle and anthem Newfoundland has been beaming up to Canada for the past twenty-five years? Now grovelling, now beseeching, now demanding, now praying?

More money, more attention, more development, more help. Equalization payments. Development grants. Special federal programmes. The older and better established parts are supposed to make a few sacrifices and send us along bundles of money and aid to help get us on the tracks.

If Newfoundland can't hope to come up to scratch and start pulling her own weight without some initial boost from the more established parts of Canada, is Labrador expected to come ahead without some aid from the Island part?

There is a great imbalance and injustice here.

Newfoundlanders here on the Island are only half alive and live only half an existence until they come to learn and realize how much that larger portion of what they call "their" country involves.

If you had to pick one word to sum up Labrador it would be *splendour*. Good God, how fresh, wide, wholesome and open it is! A person plucked off Duckworth Street or out of Piper's Hole and dropped down for the first time at Goose Airport will tremble at the knees.

So does the Bayman or the Cornerboy at his first glimpse of Young and College in Toronto. But glory in the difference. Toronto is theirs; Labrador is, or could be, ours.

Last fall, whilst an unemployed employable, I took another cruise up to Labrador to get away from it all.

By good fortune I was taken on a turn around the school at North West River. A modern school, much like any of the regional high schools on the Island, although kept in a spotless condition.

The school is for the use of the Indians who are of the tribe we know as Naskaupi. Language is the chief difficulty.

There is slow progress in formal learning because few of the teachers can speak much Naskaupi. There is much concentration on singing. At each of the classrooms the students sang a song for the visitors.

A Miss Augustine of the Phillipines is the singing teacher. I took her at first to be a Labrador native. The aboriginal people of our northern part bear a striking resemblance to the handsome races of the South Pacific.

She directed the Grade Eight class, if memory serves, to give us "Que sera, sera" or, in English, "Whatever will be, will be." They stood against the picture window of the room with the hills of Labrador behind them.

Indians singing in English and French with a slight Spanish accent. They were as pretty and they were as rich as ever they were before St. John's and Ottawa put them into tiny wooden jelly bean houses in ordered rows on the side of the bleakest hill in North West River.

Shall This Cup Pass From Us?

When do we here in the Happy Province start getting a good dash of hard times up the airholes?

Waiting for the sky to fall is getting downright tedious.

The rest of the world, according to the papers, is now suffering a combination of Armageddon, the Black Death and ten days of rainy weather.

Over in the Mother Country the times are almost as stiff as your average upper lip. In the Boston States they're cutting their grandmothers' throats for a gallon of gasoline.

What is the present government doing about our backward condition here in Newfoundland?

We are behind, as usual, like the cow's tail. How much longer must we suffer for want of some critical adversity?

Part of the trouble must be that Newfoundland has never risen high enough on the prosperity scale to suffer any great concussion from falling off it.

We now hear the piteous moans and groans from the States that a head of lettuce has gone to fifty-nine cents. Or that furnaces must be turned down from eighty degrees. Or that the speed limit is lowered to fifty-five miles per hour.

Damned tough – except you had been paying eighty cents for a bundle of green tissue paper lettuce for years, or sending older female offspring into white slavery to help pay fuel bills or had nothing to drive on but graveled caribou trails since the year one.

Over in jolly old Blighty, they're amazed at the current rate of unemployment.

Our hearts in the Happy Province go out - except we had been enjoying twenty percent out of work and a quarter of the population on the dole most winters since "good times" arrived in 1949.

One gets the feeling that the Happy Province is treading water waiting for the rest of the world to catch up.

We are running on the spot, greatly bewildered at all these reports of gloom and doom from elsewhere, while waiting for the rest of these nations to sink to our own level of deprivation.

What, this hard times? Never better, me son, never better. What looks like hard times to other more progressive parts is merely the view from the back of the hog here in Newfoundland.

Hard times to us would be having to take the mats off the floor and pitch them across the beds on chilly winters nights.

And while that might be a bit of a comedown from today it would be neither intolerable nor frightening. Even if we sank that low again it would be no more disconcerting to us than it is to prosperous states today to have to wear a sweater indoors.

Much craves more - but we never did have much. You might get a few frantic peeps from some of the hothouse plants in St. John's city.

But it is doubtful whether panic will seize, say, the southern coast of Labrador if a regulation is passed that the thermostat has to be set at sixty-eight degrees.

Mild consternation might furrow the brows of our Cabinet Ministers and glorious Leader if gas goes to one dollar a gallon catching them with ten miles per gallon cars.

But they won't be shocked too much to jack their salaries up enough to cover the difference.

From the poor man in his cottage to the rich man in his hall, the rest of the "modern" world must yet fall back to the present level of Newfoundland and below before we can really see what all the fuss is about.

Feline Heat

I'm touched to the heart by the Energy Minister's plea for "voluntary cuts" in energy consumption. As soon as his call to the colours came I plunged into serious thought. When it comes to matters of a scientific nature your average Newfoundlander's mind is like the razor's edge, so it took me only three days and nights of hard thinking to plumb the depths for the following:

It's as plain as the nose on your face that we spend one-third of our lives on the broads of our backs.

How fortuitous, then, that the coldest part of the twenty-four hours coincides with the time at night when we are generally encouched.

Now that the energy crisis is upon us we may spring immediately to the bedchamber. It simplifies matters. One-third of the day's battle with heat cuts can be fought in a conveniently smallish room.

If there is plenty of stuffing in your bedroom any heat generated there will not escape uselessly through walls and loft.

Having made things snug there, well stuffed with insulation, draft stops under the doors, et cetera, we may now turn our attention to the matter of generating heat within the bedroom.

There stands the basic enclosure, the bedchamber, ready to contain at least one uncongealed Newfoundlander for a full eight hours, but without "artificial" heating.

And so to the problem. Unthinking persons will leap to what they consider to be the obvious. They will rashly pounce upon the first method that strikes them for keeping warm under such conditions.

But, no, hot water bottles are not the answer. Think for a moment. Think. Where is the saving, where is the cut here, and with what if not oil or electricity, pray tell, is the water for those hot water bottles to be heated?

You see? We persons with a scientifical bent don't dash ourselves into logical cleft sticks like that. Rather, our first inclination would be to look into the possibility of three or four fifteen-pound tom cats.

Could not a person with three or four of these plump and substantial moggies to his back, smile, even in an otherwise unheated house, at winter's blast?

Perhaps so – perhaps not, but the theory is sound at least in principle.

A chuffy cat in its health and strength is a comfortable article with no sharp corners except some toenails which can be clipped off.

Why toms for the purpose? They run to heavier sizes than the females and three or four of a larger breed would suffice, whereas it would take from seven to ten smaller females...giving rise to complication-by-numbers with them wetting, rooting around, snarling and tissing at one another back there and so forth.

Toms are more docile, too, and except for certain seasons do not row with each other. With frost on the windows, wintry stars in the sky, your tabby backwarmers would need nothing more than a few airholes punched in the quilts to keep them content and on the job.

Of course, if a cat food crisis should next befall us the economy of the scheme is exploded. But as long as one tom cat on a can of grub a day can throw out as much heat (for this purpose) as one gallon of furnace oil, Mr. Minister can rest easy.

Let us pursue the theory still further. Ottawa is anxiously waiting, but we of the scientific community are nothing if not thorough.

The question of one sixty-pound crackie instead of four fifteen-pound tom cats arises – and, obviously, one can't have both.

By their very angularity dogs must be ruled out. Unlike your tom which is more or less circular and cushion-shaped when in repose, the dog is full of sharp angles and bones. And they root around a lot.

What is needed is something more or less padded and round,

well insulated and docile with a minimum of "elbows" sticking out.

Perhaps, indeed, one of the smaller breeds of sheep might be the ideal answer and wool is certainly an ideal warmth-conserving material and has been known as such from earliest times.

But here again, having three or four heat producing animals rather than one would be more convenient as they each could be shifted around as cold spots occurred. Besides, there are still some who would object on other grounds to a sheep between the sheets.

Some people, trying to be grander than their neighbours, will probably introduce a horse into their bedrooms with the objective of warming the whole room so they could read with their arms above the covers.

Experiment is the soul of progress but a heat-producing animal as large as a horse would give rise to many problems. For the sake of dantiness it would have to be kept tethered with its posteriors stuck out an open window.

On blustery nights, more cold air would be admitted through these open crannies than the horse would give off inside. And in no time the SPCA would probably pounce.

Turning to another angle, it is possible that some of our poorer families might consider renting out one or more of their members as backwarmers to persons sleeping in unheated houses.

If the food crisis strikes the lower orders much harder they might be quite willing to earn an extra loaf of bread for the table by offering this timely service.

Not to be indelicate about it but it might strike our bachelor readers odd that couples sharing a conjugal bed should have this heating problem at all.

One glance at a chart of the human form shows that it is absolutely impossible for two properly married persons to keep each other's backs warm...at the same time! Shape does not allow it.

Enough said. If Mr. Minister thinks he can put a battery of Ottawa physicists to work and come up with a method in advance of the fifteen-pound tom cats method he is welcome to try.

The Guy Method for Keeping Snug

For places other than the bedchamber other methods of maintaining heat must be explored. After an evening's hard thought to the problem, I have come up with the obvious solution - a solution so simple, so workable and so obvious that I expect to be met at first by cynical jeers and snickers.

Never mind. We radical thinkers are long used and hardened to such cavalier treatment.

Like all great theories, this one can be stated in baby talk.

It is an ecologically-sound method of keeping warm. Nothing is taken out of the atmosphere and nothing put in. What makes it work is the greatest little furnace ever known, the human carcass, live variety.

As every schoolboy knows, the human frame is constantly giving off heat, winter and summer. On warm days it gives off too much and we have to sweat to keep cool. On cold days, we have only to shove on a guernsey and mackinaw to keep our own heat in and are perfectly comfortable out of doors.

Carrying this scientific principle one step further, it is patently obvious that if two or more warm bodies sort of clump together the sum of heat created by them is greatly increased.

This can be clearly proven by means of trigonometry and the New Math, but we need not go into the technicalities here.

The crux of the Guy Method For Keeping Snug is that if people would abandon their present wasteful habit of moving about singly, and come together in intimate heat-producing clumps, then the Arabs could take their oil and stick it up the pyramids.

Old habits die hard. I expect that at first we will see stiff opposition to this sensible plan. But I also expect that about the middle of January coming, this last straw will be frantically snatched at.

It need hardly be said that our very first consideration must be to keep our legislators in the House of Assembly warm and in working order throughout the winter. Should this governing body seize up and their water pipes burst then there would be really no point in anyone else surviving at all.

The House is scheduled to open in January – our coldest month – and should the furnace at Conglomeration Building run out of fuel in the middle of a sitting, Newfoundland would at once slip into the chasm of doom and disaster.

Under the new Method, all forty-one of them must be moved from the chilly cavernous Chamber and stuffed into a fifteen-foot by fifteen-foot anteroom.

It is obvious at once that the amount of warmth produced in such an enclosed space would more than suffice to keep the Hon. Gents. themselves in heat while the surplus could be pumped out to warm the rest of the building.

The ruddy glow from the noses of some Hon. Gents. alone would steam up the windows in the eastern wing and if such heated parties were placed in close conjunction they could keep all the windows open in the midst of howling blizzards.

There is but one danger to this scheme. The fire commissioner would have to suggest precautions, for with the forty-one of them jammed together cheek by jowl you could get spontaneous combustion at any moment.

It might seem on the surface of it that socks which are not perfectly fresh or the scattered Hon. Gent. who was careless about personal daintiness might upset the togetherness-for-warmth scheme completely. Not so, however, as these birds have long trained themselves to endure the most horrendous stinks without so much as batting an eyelash.

As to the general laity, the same basic principles of fuel conservation could be applied.

Take, for example, the heating of public busses. All the seats could be stripped out and the passengers stuffed in, standing as thick as they could be stowed. With the friction generated among the closely-packed mass on the turns and so forth, there would be absolutely no need for a fuel-wasting bus heater.

The driver, who would still have to be seated, could be kept warm by the nearest ranks of passengers blowing on him in relays.

In the city and suburbs, persons could circumvent the need for a furnace entirely by clumping together in offices and shops during the daylight hours.

Sales clerks, for example, would move about their tasks in a solid close-packed phalanx, all in lock step with no light showing between the ranks, much as they conduct their coffee breaks right now.

In offices, the desks could be placed in a very tight circle after the manner of the musk ox when threatened, and the female secretaries placed at the centre of this tight bunch the better to radiate their warmth through the whole assemblage.

In all, I think we have in this Method nothing less than the salvation of such of the race as dwells on the cooler parts of the globe.

I'll be paying off my furnace oil man tomorrow.

Wide-Eyed and on the Move

You may have noticed that the more fashionably dressed set, both male and female, have been wearing peculiar expressions lately.

They're curiously wide-eyed and as they walk the left eye grows even wider, and then the right. It's caused by their boots.

It is all but impossible these days to buy a bit of footwear that hasn't got thick and trendy taps. As much as three inches thick in some cases. The pattern must have been taken from the dainty little slippers worn by Frankenstein's monster.

What happens to persons wearing this stylist footwear is that the great weight of the boot, as they lift the foot to take a step, drags down the skin along the whole length of the body.

This considerable strain pulls down the lower eyelid on the side which has the foot off the ground.

Hence the slightly alarming facial contortions of these modishly-shod citizens as they perambulate along in their chunkies.

But life is just one thing after another.

Last week I tried to take steps to combat the rising cost of meat.

My intentions were to see a dentist and get my teeth sharpened so that I could tackle the cheaper cuts. You need choppers like a grizzly bear to make a dent in anything you can afford these days.

But the first molar merchant I contacted set me so far back on my haunches I still haven't the nerve to try another. The earliest he could see me was next January!

There may, however, be a way out.

It seems that the Tartars, famous horsemen of the Asian plains, were in the habit of sticking a steak between their saddle and the horse's back when starting out in the morning. After bouncing about on it up hill and down dale all day, they had quite a tender chop for supper.

Could we not follow suit to our advantage? By purchasing an affordable bit of rubber cow, placing in on the driver's seat as we start off for work in the morning and deliberately hitting every pothole en route, we'd have something fairly edible for the evening meal.

In this way we'd be able to smile at both the dentists and the supermarkets, and still keep up our health and strength for when it comes time to tackle the garage.

Guy Mobile

In Advent we should be doing our best to avoid impure thoughts as the blessed Christmas season approaches.

It is not always easy.

Yesterday, for instance, I had a whole string of impure thoughts one right after the other. They occurred when my motor car broke down.

No doubt you find the idea amusing. That's the kind of bunch you are. There's nothing you find half so comical as hearing tell of other people's troubles.

So that you will get the last ounce of merriment out of my present misfortune, I must tell you that I have always been unlucky with cars. It has been a bad and traumatic history.

The first hundred feet I ever travelled while in charge of one was in reverse gear, through a substantial picket fence and down over a six-foot dump.

The shock of the upset was not nearly as great as my surprise at the relative calm with which my father received the news.

In later years, properly licenced and authorized, I fell into ownership (might as well name names) of something called a "Chevy II."

This was one of the first of the compacts, a staid, no-nonsense vehicle generally regarded as appropriate transportation for retired gentlefolk and something I couldn't go wrong in even if I tried, they said.

I can't honestly fault that machine. It was about the time, as you may recall, that we were seized with the universal and burning determination to finish the drive in '65, thanks to Mr. Pearson.

The Chevy II was finished about the same time the highway was.

Next, true to form, I acquired a Corvair and two months later Ralph Nadar announced that they were four-wheeled death traps.

Perhaps the chance of being strung up through the telephone wires on tricky turns added extra spice to the Corvair but I found it a most enjoyable touring machine.

Only hitch was that the mufflers cost ninety dollars a pair and dropped off once a forthnight, the engine and transmission had to be removed if you want to change the spark plugs, and the gas gauge showed anything from a quarter to three parts full when the tank was actually bone dry.

It was altogether too exotic for local mechanics. I ended up trying to outguess the gas gauge and walked miles in all weathers fair and foul; I found that two coat hangers secured the mufflers at least a week longer than the garage could.

In desperation, I then turned to the clever Japanese.

Apart from a slipping fan belt one evening while touring the Florida Keys, the Datsun was far less inscrutable than the Corvair and hummed merrily along without a hitch for two years.

Then it fell apart all at once, rather like the Deacon's wonderful one-horse shay.

I was driving along one day when the back of the driver's seat collapsed flat. I grabbed for the door handle to upright myself and it came out by the roots, and the clutch apparently dropped dead with fright.

Matters really came to a head one brisk day last March. The gas cap had a lock which opened with the ignition key. That day, the gas station chap came back around to the window holding the broken stump of my one and only key in his mitt.

They had hysterics back at the Datsun dealership when I phoned to ask the chances of getting a duplicate key.

They near bust a gut laughing at the impossibility of such a request. For, by this time, the dealer I had bought the little oriental marvel from had gone out of business, another garage had taken them but no longer carried them, and the third lot of chaps now were taking a crack at it.

So you ended up being treated as if you had the car owner's equivalent of leprosy.

I won't mention any names. They'll get no free advertising off me. But on that brisk day last March (and March was unexcelled for days of surpassing briskness) as I stood among the wreckage of the Datsun entertaining impure thoughts, I knew I had come to the end of my tether at last.

I made a sudden lunge for the telephone and rang the distributors for a certain brand of car famed for its ruggedness, its dependability, its solidity and its ability to muck around for an average of eleven years in Lapland winters without a hitch.

"Come and get me!" I cried into the telephone, my voice breaking with emotion. "Come and take me out of this and I'll buy one of your cars on the spot."

So I did.

I felt secure in a motor car for the first time in my life. They use devilishly clever propaganda in their advertising and I had swallowed it; hook, line and sinker.

My brainwashing was so complete that two months later when an accelerator spring snapped off in a sixty-mile-per-hour zone and left the engine roaring out of control I put my faith in the no less than three separate braking systems – and made allowances.

Actually used to pity the poor unfortunates who had to risk their necks daily in tin cans from Oshawa and Detroit.

Pride goeth before a fall and a haughty spirit before destruction.

Because yesterday I had to get towed to a service station feet first. It must be the ultimate in humiliation. I turned up my collars and slouched as low in the seat as I could.

At the garage they said it was a queer thing. They said it was an uncommon thing, an unusual thing. They couldn't figure why it was she conked out, without keeping her in overnight for observation.

Which left me to walk the thirteen miles home, take a taxi, or engage a room on Brazil Square for the night.

A Changed Man

Evil spirits is what it was.

Yes, it was evil spirits that got into my motor car and caused me all the trouble.

The hand of man, either on the assembly line or in the garage, had absolutely nothing whatsoever to do with it.

If ever a bad word escaped my lips regarding Swedish motor cars or the local agents thereof, I am thoroughly ashamed.

It was solely the work of evil spirits.

A change, as you can clearly see, has come over me. I am a reformed person. I am not the man I once was. Something happened to turn me around in my tracks, purge me of every last drop of nastiness, and reduce me to the basically sweet person I used to be.

Whereas it took three separate spirits to effect a similar change in Mr. Dickens' Scrooge, it has taken only a garage bill to convert me.

What a miserable wretch was I! What a Scrooge to grumble so!

It was, as I say, the bill that did it.

Having been deprived of my conveyance for twenty-four hours I went around to the garage yesterday to collect it. I was in foul spirits, and Christian Charity was not in me.

So far the breakdown of my new motor car had cost me ten dollars for a tow and start, nineteen dollars in taxi fares, two-and-a-half hours standing around a service station in a chill factor of minus twenty, and a good dose of the flu.

Now I was prepared to receive the full heft of a garage bill squarely on the chin.

I have never known a garage bill yet to be less than $38.95, tax included. That seems to be the generally accepted minimum for garage bills. For that price they'll kick your tires, empty your ashtrays and tap your carburetor with the handle of a screwdriver.

You may appreciate my speechless condition, then, when I drew the fearsome yellow sheet toward me through the wicket and read in the final, ultimate, grand-slam "TOTAL AMOUNT," where your whole life usually flashes in front of your eyes, the figure fifty-four cents!

One single item on all that great yellow expanse. Part Number 21515428 – Gasoline Anti Freeze, 54 cents. For the moment I thought either I had been struck blind on the spot or else they had put the heavy stuff in little tiny print.

But nothing! Nothing under shop labour. Body shop labour was empty. Parts was vacant. Gas, oil, and grease was bare. Sub-let labour was devoid of figures. Accessories was as bare as a baby's bottom. Special work contained not a blemish. Sundries had never seen the imprint of a ballpoint pen.

"Probably just some condensation got into your gasoline," said a kindly mechanic, clapping me on the back. "Nothing serious."

"Glory to God in the Highest!" I thought, but was in such transports of relief that not a sound escaped my lips. "Praise to the Holiest in the heights that it was nothing serious!"

It is at such sacred moments of deliverance as that that you hear the angelic choirs tuning up in the distance.

Restored to wheels once more, I climbed into my faithful Scandinavian masterpiece and drove down, enraptured, toward my place of employment with my heart beating like a little jingle bell.

Colleagues must have sensed almost at once the great change that had come over me.

"God bless us every one!" I cried, skipping blithely toward the window that overlooks Duckpuddle Street. "Ho, boy! Yes, you down there! Do you know that big goose that hangs in the window on the corner?" I asked the rosy-cheeked lad on the sidewalk. "Nip round there at once and tell them to put it on my bill and send it up to the garage.

Be back here in five minutes and you shall have a bright, shining farthing."

"Lay off, you condemned fruit cake," responded the little lad below, "or I'll call the cops."

"Clever lad!" I cried, raising my finger in reciprocal salute. "Bright lad! A more splendid little hub-cap nicker was never born!"

For now that I have become a changed person I cannot find it in my heart to be nasty or mean to anyone.

I intend to make amends. I propose to make up for lost time. Hardly a day will pass over my head that I won't sing the praises of roadside restaurants, garages, government PR men, timid editors, the Holy City of St. John's, clergymen, politicians, resettlers, Christmas advertisers, sociologists, anthropologists, open-line hosts, Canada, other drivers, alien do-gooders, hot turkey sandwiches, and maggotty-headed young layabouts.

Oh, say it is not too late!

A Few Passages from Unholy Writ

It was the middle of July, 1971, the start of the Dog Days, and poor Mr. Smallwood had gone up to Labrador to open the Mighty Churchill; to throw a switch creating the new Smallwood Lake..."six times larger, Mr. Speaker, than the Sea of Galilee...."

CHAPTER I

(Joseph setteth forth out of the Kingdom of Joe; he remarketh upon the surpassing smallness of the brain pans of they that dwell therein; and maketh merry.)

1. And it came to pass in those days that in the seventh month Joseph gathered together all the scribes and high priests and they that were exceedingly brown of nose; and did pass out of the Kingdom of Joe into that part which is called Lab-Rador meaning the Land Joe Gave to Doyle.
2. And he ascended into the heavens and sitteth up front in first class: Yea, even as he passeth over the Kingdom of Joe he looketh down as from an mighty cloud and partook of an little Jerez and spake thus:
3. Behold, O ye congregation of hangers on; we passeth hence over an exceedingly stunned people; Rejoice, O ye followers and disciples;

4. For verily I say unto you that inasmuch as they seemeth not to know bee from an bull's hoof thereby do we live and breathe and have our being; for let stunnedness pass from the Kingdom of Joe and we shall be all undone even like unto a draft of gutted haddocks.

5. But fear not for in stunnedness they were conceived and in darkness and superstition do they travail from generation to generation;

6. And Joseph did speak further unto them that were with him saying: Who can tell what manner of people they be that supporteth us from generation even unto generation?

7. And they that were with him were sore perplexed and opened not their lips; and Joseph said unto them: Verily, I say unto you, they are like unto a manner of people that falleth to the ground and misseth.

8. When they heard these words, they made exceeding merry and smote their knees and smote each one the other upon the back; loud was their exultation at the wisdom of Joseph even like unto an great company of larks.

9. And some there were that partook of an other drop for their stomach's sake; and some that pincheth the comely handmaidens which passeth out drink and victuals and Halifax Chronicles upon the winged chariots of Epa;

10. And so it was that they passed over the Kingdom of Joe and into that part which is called Lab-Rador.

CHAPTER II

(Joseph pauseth by the waters of Churchill and Vieweth the land; he putteth the two tribes an half in mind of his promise to them and prophesieth a restoration of the scattered flock.)

1. There was in the same land of Lab-Rador an certain geological engineer who was of the tribe Kebek; who did sit in the house of an publican by the waters of Churchill sipping an beverage; and they that sat with him sipped also;

2. And suddenly, a messenger appeared crying: Behold, the bridegroom cometh like unto a mighty rushing wind; and they that heard it sprang up and headeth for the landing strip: Yea, even unto the very asphalt thereof.

3. And Joseph arose and passed forth upon the tarmac and the multitudes parted and he passed through the midst; then went he forthwith into the tents of the tribe of Brinco and unlatched the sandals of his feet.

4. And they of the tribe of Brinco were like unto an cat upon hotted bricks for well they knew of the vagaries of Joseph.

5. So it came to pass that on the day appointed Joseph and all the scribes and high priests and they that were exceeding brown of nose together with the chiefs of the tribe of Brinco went forth even unto the waters of Churchill,

6. And he went up into a little hill and spake in this wise unto the assembled multitudes:

7. Verily, verily, I say onto you, O ye Pharasees and Saducees and ye supervisory personnel of the land of Kebek; know ye that I am the king of all these lands anointed by the Lord to rule over them even unto the end of time;

8. For though I am great in years, verily am I also yet great in lip and chipper like unto the cricket; yea, even as the grasshopper that suffereth not the grass to grow under the sole of her foot ere she skippeth apace again, so even is the ruler of the Kingdom of Joe.

9. For, low, he that keepeth watch over Bison Petroleum shall not slumber nor sleep; and he that watcheth over Shaheen Enterprises shall not slip neither shall he fall; and let them that are of the tribe of dirty Tories put that in their pipe even as it smoketh.

10. He that voteth for the dirty Tories shall be cut down and his house shall be scattered about the land even as the turds of an spavined camel.

11. He that so transgresseth against the covenant of Joseph even though he now waxeth fat upon long term assistance shall be rooted out; and he that selleth wine in the marketplace shall be laid low.

12. And all that were there marvelled at these things and they that were of the land of Kebek said one to another, Tabernac: which meaneth in the tongue of that country, Surely, Duplessis is still among us;

13. When Joseph heard the multitudes murmuring in this wise he saith unto himself: Verily, that which hath cut ice for lo this

full score of years and two cutteth no ice here; and he taketh an other tack.

14. And he spake saying, I speak to you of many signs and wonders; and he prosphesied of exceeding great vessels to be builded in the Town of Mary and stretched forth his arms; even as one who proclaimeth the length of the one that getteth away.

15. And spake he then of an mighty sea of oil of such abundance that an foolish virgin caught with lamp yet untrimmed shall forthwith lose her status; and of many other exceeding great prophesies prophesied he them.

CHAPTER III

(He causeth the waters to overflow the land; of them that shall be consumed; the flight out of Lab-Rador.)

1. When Joseph had finished speaking he came down from the hillside and all that were there followed him even unto the shores of Lobstick; and when he was there he lifteth up his arms crying in a loud voice:

2. He that hath brought orange juice out of the land of Panama and hath commanded hockey sticks to be builded upon the fields of Harmon shall cause the waters to overflow the land.

3. And all they that saw it were sore amazed; and the waters over-flowed the land even an hundred cubits to the westward.

4. So that even they which dwelth in the City of Montreal in the land of Kebek were smitten with flooded basements.

5. Then spake Joe saying, Verily, O ye that dwelleth in the land of Kebek, fear not for I shall give ye an attractive offer on an exceeding great ark to be builded in the Town of Mary in the kingdom of Joe so that ye may escape the tumult of waters;

6. And such as were there who were of the land of Kebek rose up for they were exceeding sore; and did rail against the tribe of Joseph even as they puncheth them in the chops.

7. So Joseph and his brethren did flee the land of Lab-Rador; and ascended once more into heaven; and Joseph ordereth an stiff belt of Jerez and worried not that he thus offendeth such as were present of the sons of the pentecost and sayeth,

8. Curst be he that first inventeth the polling booth: for if we sucketh them in an seventh time it shall be an exceeding great miracle. Yea, Verily.

The Poor We Have With Us Always

It is funny how the infant mind functions.

I can mind, when I was small, being lodged off down on the coats in the back of the school at dances.

This is where they put you at about two o'clock in the night when you commenced to get groggy and wanted a nap. There was a row of desks shoved in tight to the wall for all hands to put their coats on. Sometimes there would be three or four of us at once laid out heads and tails down there, some on a half-doze, more with their thumbs stuck in their gobs looking around, and others a cold junk sleeping it off.

Solid comfort.

I can recall hearing this very restful "RUMP-A-RUMP-A-RUMP" noise in the background. It was half a shuffle and half a stamp which caused the floor to heave rhythmically and rattle a few loose panes in the windows.

And I remember watching the light from the kerosene oil lamps dancing on the ceiling from the draft as they all swung around in the Reel, and I can remember a strange noise threading through everything, rising and falling in tune with the flickering light.

The big puzzle occupying my infant noggin was: Is that noise making the light or is that light making the noise?

This is the first thing I can remember about times.

Of course, before many more years had passed I had put two and two together and figured out that the noise was coming from the fiddler who was playing an accordian. He was always called the fiddler regardless of what he played upon.

First they would have the Sale of Work. Second, they had the First Table followed by the Second and Third Tables depending on how many were there. Then they might have a Guess Cake or Grab Bags, and third they had the Dance.

Sale of Work was cloths and aprons and pillow slips hung across on lines, and all worked out into cock sparrows and roses; and double mitts, fancy for Sundays; and cushion tops all made mostly out of dyed wool and flour bags bleached out.

You never saw many figgy buns flung about at the First Table. There was always a steadier lot sitting in at it. They even had grace at First Table, which had to do for Second and Third Tables too where you had more driving works and carrying on.

They used to sing grace.

Every word was stretched out to the extent of an elastic garter. It was the most dismal thing you ever heard. "Beeeeee prezzzzz-ent aaayt oour taaaay-ble, Lord" and so on through, "Be here and everywhere adored; Thy creatures bless and grant that we; May feast in Paradise with Thee. AAAAAAWWWWWMMMMMENNNNNNNNN."

Then the Catholics from Southern Harbour blessed theirselves and all hands sat down and dug in.

Generally, they had Meat Teas or Soup Suppers.

This was bully beef and potato salad of different sorts. Then jelly and blanc mange and partridge berry tarts and cakes and figgy buns and tea.

If someone who had a few drinks in, or some of the youngsters, hove a bun at someone at the other end of the table or flicked blanc mange on their spoons across, then one of the women serving on the table would give them a click across the ear and tell them to behave the same as they ought.

When they had Soup Suppers you got a chance to be sent down to the house for the boiler.

Halfways up with it yourself and the other chap put down the boiler, took off the cover and drove your arm down to rummage a biggish bit of meat off the bottom.

This was a tricky business.

You had to be quick because they were timing you back at the school. If you took too much they would notice it because meat wasn't that plentiful. And the stuff was burning hot.

So it was in and out of the boiler as quick as you could and then jam your arm down in the snow to take the sting out. Once, Gordon lost his mitt in the boiler and forgot to hook it out and got a lacing for it.

When the Last Table was nearly eat down to a shambles, they started the dance.

Mostly they had sets which included such things as "Form a Line and Advance," "Dance to Your Partner" and "Round the House." Sometimes they had "the Reel" or the "Furginia Reel" and, in later years, a "Wallace."

Everyone got out except for the small youngsters and women not feeling well. The oldish men were always the ring leaders of it.

There were two sides to a set and when one side stopped the other side commenced. To my knowledge, there is no harder or faster or longer dancing in the world unless among uncivilized races.

The windows were up with the snow blowing in, the door was open, the stove was let die down. But whenever the fiddler stopped, the men in their shirtsleeves with sweat running down their backs would lurch for the door and fall across the bridge rail outside, with the steam flying out of them in the frost.

And the women panting for breath with their hands to their bosoms would stagger off toward the kitchen to dip a cup in the water barrel. They would shake their heads to the other women in the kitchen and puff their cheeks and say, "Ohmygod! I'm just about dead."

The Reel was even worse. When someone would mention having the Reel there would be groans all around and people saying, "Oh, no, not the Reel. For God's sake not the Reel." Reels took an hour or more apiece.

As a lad I was somewhat on the slight side. It is only these late years that I have fallen into flesh. So one of my worries then was that a woman might take me off my feet in the dances.

Some of them were upwards of seventeen stone. There were very few there that any husky man could swing off their feet, so generally it worked out to be a tie. But imagine getting taken off your feet yourself!

When you got swinging about 102 miles an hour they commenced to tighten their grip until you could feel your ribs lap over and your draft cut off and see little spots dancing in front of your eyes.

If two people swinging happened to rouse into two more, some bad injuries were likely to result. If you let go at top speed you would clear the floor like an oblong bowling ball and probably have to be dug out of the wall.

Only the poorest kind of dances ever finished up before it was daylight all abroad.

By means of these affairs they built schools, churches and halls, assisted distressed persons, sent parcels overseas and helped put a stitch of clothes on the poor naked backs of heathens in other countries who, although odd looking, are created in our blessed Saviour's image just the very same as you and me.

Once when I was telling a person from upalong about Soup Suppers and so forth he shook his head and became down in the mouth and said: "You must have been very poor."

Strange talk. If we had been poor it would have been the other way around. People in other countries would have been running off Soup Suppers to send parcels over to us.

It is funny how the mainland mind functions.

Ottawa

In December of sixty-nine I spent a few days in the beautiful capital city of Ottawa where the carefree natives bask in the balmy breezes howling down off the tundra and happiness is when your longjohns don't bunch.

I had intended to make the rounds early to try to find out where it's at. Unfortunately, I was under orders to go along and see what went on at the House of Commons.

So I strapped on my snowshoes and pushed along to Parliament Hill.

There's this mess of buildings standing on a rise above the river, you understand, and they're made out of rocks that have been roughly squared off and piled one atop the other. No kidding. They have all the architectural grace of abandoned root cellars.

The roofs of these buildings are made up of all sorts of peaks and nooks and towers and wings and flutes and outgrowths and the whole thing has been sheathed over with copper which has turned the colour of a jungle fungus.

And on top of this again there's a weird collection of iron scroll-work that looks like the aftermath of a fire in a coathanger factory. Altogether it's one of the most incredible collections of buildings outside the fishing stages at Pushthrough.

Up over the front door they have a snatch of verse carved in the rocks: "The wholesome sea is at her gates, her gates both east and west." Well, I don't know too much about the west but there's parts in the east that aren't too bloody wholesome these days.

The first thing I did once inside was to look for the cobwebs. Inside the premises the layout is even freakier, if possible, than the outside. There are these high churchy ceilings with arches and knick-knacks all over the place. Bat paradise.

And, I'm happy to report, the cobwebs were still there. It gives you a sense of stability, something to hang on to in these changing times. I first noticed the cobwebs almost a year before – a big swag of them just inside the door and to the right.

Anyhow, it being two o'clock, I proceeded on to the Commons Chamber where the question period was about to start. What a place. Spooks and ghosts, creaking doors, walking dead, the Moors, Heathcliffe, the wreck of the Hesperus. A most depressing sight is the Commons Chamber.

Well, there were a couple of our chaps down there on the PC side, although our man in the government seemed to be absent. The name of the game seemed to be to groan when someone on the other side made a wisecrack and to pound your desk when somebody on your side did.

One chap asked about Canada's position on the latest bit of buchery in Viet Nam, and was answered by a statement guaranteed to give you the dry heaves.

They were asking if Canada would take in the Jews who were leaving Poland, what was being done about the wheat markets and whether or not the price of French pastry should be put under some form of government control. Was the government thinking of building wheat storage elevators in Newfoundland? There was a strangling noise over in one corner that sounded like somebody bolted his upper plate.

I can't dwell on any more of that scene. It's too gruesome.

When it was over the spectators and the press and most of the members down on the floor jumped up and made for the door. They couldn't hack it any longer.

Outside in the sub-Arctic air again I stopped for a few minutes as usual at the statue of Her Late Majesty which is on a prominent rise to the right as you come out. You're the only swinger in Ottawa, madam.

Having discharged this painful duty I was now free to circulate about the city and find out where it's at. I finally found it – just down the corridor and to your right. And you had to pay ten cents to get in.

The next day I had to leave Ottawa and head either east or west. If I'd had a coin left I would've flipped it. One thing sure, whichever way you turn up there you run into Newfoundland immigrants.

Half the population of Kumquat Quay has probably ended up in Moose Jaw. Branding cats. No trouble to feel at home from one end of the country to the other.

So I really don't know why all of them live on spaghetti to save enough to try to get back to Newfoundland for Christmas.

Christmas in the Bay

In the last week of Advent the house smelled like a forest.

Behind the kitchen stove, stacked as neatly as books on library shelves, was a wall of firewood. Some junks of dry and weathered rampikes but most of sappy spruce and balsam fir with turpentine bladders and green twigs sticking off.

The heat from the stove brought out the smell. Out in the porch there were firewood reinforcements. The woodbox was full; it was piled high at both ends.

In all, there was enough firewood in the house and ready to do, along with a few scuttles of coal, for twelve days and twelve nights.

Some say the artificial Christmas trees are a disappointment because there's no smell on them. In the mid-nineteen-forties, Christms trees were still uncommon out around the bay but you wouldn't have noticed the smell of one anyway for the aroma off the twelve-day's supply of firewood.

The kitchen stove was the only source of heat in the house. It was allowed to die out at night and was relit each morning with splits and shavings.

Indeed, people passed every night of the winter in uninsulated houses with no fire, no storm windows. If it was minus ten degrees out of doors, by morning it could be minus ten degrees in the bedrooms.

They kept warm on mattresses stuffed with the feathers and down of chickens and wild birds, covered over with quilts and comforters stuffed with wool.

Now we have a fuel crisis and great countries are plunged into distress because thermostats have to be turned down to sixty-eight degrees.

Christmas lasted a whole twelve days then. It was the most remarkable celebration of the year. Even weddings did not come close to it.

Everything possible was done to see that work was cut to a bare minimum during these twelve days. Enough firewood was in and the water-barrels in the porch brimmed full of water from the well.

All the laundry, baking, scrubbing, butchering, brewing, polishing, mending, patching and cleaning had been done until seven days into the New Year.

There was little work to be done in Christmas except to shovel the drifts from the door in the morning and feed the hens, sheep, horse and cow in the evening.

Christmas now is a glorified weekend. People then apparently determined to give themselves the whole twelve days because they knew they needed it. It was not coincidence that a hard-working people gave themselves the longest break of the year at such a time.

It is the darkest time of year; the long, hard winter stretches ahead. So why not shatter the darkness and gloom with a glorious bash that was the highlight of the year in those times and would be impossible to achieve in today's society.

Considering the circumstances, Christmas then was a heroically defiant thing, a blaze of light hurled by puny men against the longest night; a brazen riotous celebration to say that in the midst of darkness the Saviour was born and the people would live through the cold, both in body and soul.

It was a most positive and optimistic thing.

During those twelve days people would do things they wouldn't dream of doing during the rest of the year.

For instance, they got drunk. Well, not "drunk" as the word means today, but they had "a drop in." Respectable, stern, sober pillars of the church had to be helped home once or twice through Christmas along the slippery roads by boys holding them up and they beaming happily and misplacing their feet as if they were the very lords of misrule.

But people said, "Oh, well, 'tis Christmas, you know." It was just not done to even recall in July that these stern old greyhairs had danced so wild in the reels on St. Stephen's Day.

The turkey wasn't invented yet but there were rabbits in the bakepot and turrs in the oven. There were fowls stewed tender with onions and stuffing and the carcass of a lamb or pig hanging down in the store over the water where it would keep.

There were ducks and geese and venison and salt water birds. There were herring and potatoes and bread. There was jam yesterday, today and tomorrow. There were candies and brew and brandy from St. Peter's.

And there was rum washed out of rum puncheons and wine in bottles from Madeira. There was lots of church, and the poles with the kerosene lamps on them on both sides of the aisle were wrapped in evergreen boughs and tissue-paper roses.

If there was snow there was lots of coming down hills on all sorts of slides in the nights when the moon was bright as day.

There were all the men and boys playing football with a blown-up pig's bladder covered over and stitched with sail canvas.

There was everything. There was everything for everybody.

And the old ladies said, well, perhaps they would, since it was Christmas, have just a little stain, just a little small stain for their stomach's sake and... Oh, my it made them right giddy-headed, ha, ha.

On New Years night the church bell would ring and all the guns fired off just like at a wedding because, I suppose, they were taking another New Year for better for worse, for richer or poorer, in sicknesa and in health....

And Old Christmas Day was almost as good as Christmas Day except a little smaller and it was said you could go up to the stable at twelve o'clock in the night and hear the beasts talk.

Then that was it for another year and it was a good thing.

In Praise of Snow

The main difference between youngsters and older persons is that while one lot likes the snow, the other would sooner see the devil coming.

Youngsters, speaking from memory, could never get enough of snow. This is due to something wrong with their heads. They don't look forward like we do.

If it is in the heights of the Dog Days in July, that suits them to a "T"; and if it is a raging blizzard in February, they don't wish for anything better.

When they grow up and get better sense they try to hasten along the winters by thinking about their summer holidays, and when summer comes they don't enjoy it because of the thought that fall and winter follow.

But youngsters, having childish minds, are perfectly content with what they see out the window in the mornings. Not only content, but eager to get out into it. If they didn't grow out of this immature attitude as time passed, there'd be no place for them but the Lunatic Asylum.

However, while they are youngsters they may enjoy snow from start to finish.

That first sprinkle of beady stuff one day in November, seed pearls far whiter than wedding rice fallng on the mud, just about drives them cracked.

And that last swirl of huge flakes in May, with a large warm sun shining through all and making a dazzling maze in the air, no less sends them out of their little noggins with joy.

Youngsters don't catch on very fast.

Time seems to pass so slowly for them between May and November they forget entirely what snow looks like.

When the first shower of winter comes they look out the window with their little gobs hanging open, struck dumb with amazement. They might as well be little blacks from the African jungle suddenly plunked down on Greenland's icy mountains.

They think it the greatest miracle that ever was to see the whole world white as paper whilst older persons, having better sense, say, "O, Gosh, here we go again!"

Even when they are eight or ten and it happens again they step out the back door all bundled up like the men in the moon stepping down.

They make little prods at it with their shovels to see if it is hard or soft. They stick the top of their mitt into it and pick some up and taste it. Then they flop right down on their gut and roll around in it.

If me or you did that there'd be talk.

The trouble with youngsters is that they don't seem to have any more memory than a person 110 years of age. No, not as much.

Because, up to a certain age, they behave in the same silly fashion over the first blades of grass to come out of the ground in the spring as they do when the first shower of snow rattles down in the fall.

Anyway, there is no doubt that, with regard to snow, youngsters have a long way to go before they get common sense.

A fact sometimes overlooked by older persons is that snowballs can't be made every day of the week, not by a long shot. It is only a very scattered time that conditions are absolutely perfect. On dry, frosty days you might as well try to make them out of flour and on mauzy, soppy days all you'll do is get your mitts wringing wet.

But there are days when the substance is exactly right. So right that you go around for hours patting one in your hands, squeezing it between your knees and patting it some more, bound on making the roundest, hardest, most perfect snowball there ever was in the world.

The first thing to do is to whack one up in the side of the house.

It makes a lovely sound. Then you can chuck a half dozen or so at telephone poles. But after that you have got to go and look for someone else to chuck them at.

It is wicked, wicked, wicked to put rocks in snowballs. It is even more wicked than just chucking rocks alone in the summertime. It is just about the wickedest thing that anyone can do. Not only is it un-Christian, but, further, it is un-Church of England. It makes no difference what the other bunch does. They don't know no better. But if I ever hear tell of you putting rocks in snowballs....

Not only would your Father in Heaven get you for putting rocks in snowballs but so would your father at the breakfast table, and what you wouldn't get then is supper.

I do know of instances of a person putting rocks in snowballs but then everyone else used to gang up on him but still had a hard job driving him over the road. And his father was the sexton.

When we would have him nearly turned tail he would come to the last ditch.... "I'm puttin' a cliffty rock in this one!" he would shout. We all knew how sharp a cliffty rock is on the corners as compared to a round, beachy one.

But, generally, everyone would heave snowballs at each other until their arms were hove out of socket a foot and they'd make great taffy pullers.

Sometimes we would make a batch and throw a bucket of water over them and leave them overnight. No rocks, mind you. Just lumps of ice like the iron. But this never worked. There is no satisfaction in throwing them as they slip around in your mitts and fly off in all directions. Nothing beats the ordinary snowball.

Life is too short to tell about randying.

You could randy on anything. Bits of old floor canvas and pieces of cardboard boxes. Stave slides which your father made out of old barrels. Made slides and coasters, hand slides and catamarans, toboggans and even a person's plain stomach.

Taking off down the hill and everyone trying to jump aboard and everyone aboard trying to knock him off.

Going like the shot when the hill was icy. Let out after supper on bright nights when the moon was bright as day and rattling down the hill like the rocket with the sparks flying off when the runners grazed the rocks.

Headed straight for the fence at ten thousand miles an hour and not being able to stop. Then grabbing the coaster and running like heck before they popped out the door when they heard the pickets crack.

Even so slight a thing as a very thin bit of snow falling on the patch of ice in the meadow was useful. You could make a run and skate the length of it on your boots, sideways.

When it was just right you could roll up a ball of snow so big that no one could push it - roll it up like a jellyroll leaving the bare ground behind and bits of old grass and twigs and sheep's buttons stuck into your ball of snow.

If there were drifts you could make tunnels through them, or, if there was someone in the tunnels, get up on top and jump it all down on them.

There was more than one kind of snow then.

Don't Cry – It Doesn't Matter

Nothing cheers your average Newfoundlander half so much as mucking about in doleful exercises like federal elections.

He is never in brisker spirits than when wallowing along after such a melancholy, boring, moth-eaten carnival as now is dragging to its petrified conclusion.

Any other normal, sane, sensible member of the human race would just as soon be in hell with his back broke as have to listen to five minutes of it.

But I bet there'll be hundreds, if not thousands, trotting along to the polls on Monday to mark an "X" for one or the other of these twenty-odd hopefuls who are eager to get out of Newfoundland while the going is good.

Despite the efforts of their hired PR hacks to sell them on TV like arm-pit spray or eighteen percent loans, they remain a nameless faceless bundle of nothing.

Their commercials looked so much like the ones for washing powders and floor wax that everyone ignored them as usual and went to the bathroom or out by the clapboard while they were on.

Name me, can you, right off the bat and no hesitation, just half of the twenty-odd who'd like to settle down in Ottawa before the winter sets in?

Canadian elections should be left to Canadians.

We've got enough pig-sticking contests of our own right here.

The best vote in this election is no vote at all.

No matter how you look at it.

They might, if they see there's no votes coming in from Newfoundland, get excited and send us down bigger parcels of money.

Better still, they might go about their business and leave us alone.

For what little entertainment we got out of the election none of these birds deserves a vote. That's the only thing you get out of elections in the long run – a few laughs while these nut cases are running and dashing about cutting each other's throats.

You may feel it's worth the effort just to get at least seven of these jokers out of Newfoundland and settled away in a nice house in Ottawa.

But they won't guarantee us they'll stay away.

Chances are that in a few years time they'll be back here inflicting themselves on us again.

Don't vote – it only encourages them.

Alas, I dare say there'll be too few followiwng this valuable advice At this stage of the game, in the fourth election inside of twelve months, voting has probably become a habit in Newfoundland.

Anyway, there it is.

You have the best suggestion I can come up with for giving this election that extra little Newfie twist those Canadians have come to expect from us.

If you choose to ignore it and vote anyway, go ahead.

It's your funeral.

Ha, ha, ha.

Next to Nothing at All

What's goin' on?

A question that many people are asking these days but one more easily asked than answered.

In an effort to find out what's going on I eavesdropped on two persons in a restaurant yesterday.

Talking to a friend from around the bay was a resident of the city:
"What's goin' on out your way? Anything...or what?"

"Nothing, boy, nothing."

"Nothing at all, eh?"

"No, nothing at all. Well, no. Not nothing at all but next to nothing at all. What's goin' on in here. Anything at all?"

"Nothing, boy. Well, little or nothing. Let's put it this way...there is and there isn't."

"Not much going on anywhere, seems like. Well, I suppose there is a bit going on here and there, but nothing here. Nothing at all."

So it seems that what's going on is nothing at all. Or very little. Hardly enough, apparently, to keep the mind alive.

Guy's Estate

(A scion of Reid, the railroad builder, had claimed he owned nearly one-tenth of the Island.)

I own the Avalon Peninsula.

I'm serving notice here and now to all these illegal squatters from one end of the Avalon Peninsula to the other to vacate the premises.

Everybody out. You have exactly a fortnight to pack your goods and chattels and haul your backsides up over the Isthmus. This is, I think, quite reasonable under the circumstances.

It was only last fall that I discovered that I owned the Avalon.

Some old papers came into my possession in September past. The claim dates back, of course, to 1610 when John Guy Esq. was given it by no less a personage than Our Dread Sovereign Lord, James I.

Put that in your pipe and smoke it...but don't chuck any messy old matches around to dirty up the property!

It has taken me since then to straighten out a few minor legal details. French claims at Placentia and environs, for instance. But I find that your avaricious Frenchman hasn't got a leg to stand on.

They were well and truly trounced away back and, if the Magna Carta and the Battle of Foxtrap are anything to go by, a damn good trouncing is nine-tenths of the law.

Then there was the little matter of sub-letting a few bits of The Guy Estate (as it is properly known) way back, to Lord Faulkland and Lord Baltimore.

That has all been taken care of. I have located the direct descendants of Faulkland and Baltimore over in the Old Country and Reggie and Stinks - as I call them - proved to be most reasonable.

All Reggie wants is an invitation for the grousing on Trepassey Barrens every other year, while Stinks, the Ninth Lord Baltimore, made the mistake of engaging me in a little game of cards.

St. John's proved to be the biggest hitch. Apparently it was left out of the original Guy Estate, probably on sanitary grounds - so I am stuck with a little enclave here on the northeast corner.

What to do with it? I am prepared to dicker. The exact terms are still being worked out but I should think that somewhere in the neighbourhood of ten cents per flush per water closet in perpetuity would be acceptable.

Should City Fathers prove to be baulky over this paltry and reasonable demand, I believe I can promise a nasty little surprise to any St. John's resident who tries to venture out beyond the Donovan's Overpass.

Trespassers will be prosecuted.

With real estate the price it is today, it is better to hold on to these bits of land after having cleared them of squatters and other undesirable wildlife.

Of course, some sharp real estate agent might catch me in a bargaining mood some year - particularly about the end of March.

I might, under these circumstances, be prepared to swap the Avalon for one of the Lesser Antilles providing, of course, that the Flush Fee of St. John's be chucked into the deal to sweeten the pot.

Meanwhile, the management of a large estate entails many headaches.

How to dispose, for instance, of the federal and provincial members now "respresenting" the so-called Avalon Peninsula? I am thinking of keeping them on. They have certain talents and might do as Flush Fee Collectors.

Decisions, decisions.

While I have tried to keep the transaction fairly secret until today, I believe there has been a leak.

The Premier is, I understand, making rather feverish attempts to sell his house in Carbonear. No doubt he thought he would be away and clear before I could make my move.

However, he is getting the same notice as everyone else – exactly a fortnight to scrape together what he can carry on his back and to dust his heels for the other side of the Isthmus.

If any of these government chaps think they can seek refuge within the St. John's enclave they have another think coming. For them the Flush Fee alone would be prohibitive.

Whatever is left of the scratch and dent sale at Come By Chance, and by the phosphorus kids at Long Harbour, will be shipped off to New York and London, respectively, at their own expense.

There's a lot of tidying up to do as the grounds have been left in a scandalous state.

I anticipate some outcry from bleeding hearts in other quarters.

You can almost hear them now.

"What an ogre! Just because he owns the Avalon Peninsula he is kicking all the people off. It should be taken to the United Nations or at least heard before the Magistrate's Court!"

That is just so much wee-weeing into the wind.

Through the years these illegal squatters firmly believed they owned the land they were living on, yet what interest did they show in it?

None whatsoever, sir. They allowed themselves to be shoved around and robbed and gypped and made fools of by every sleeveen that came down the road and were never happier than when governed by rogues and traitors who gave their Country away bit by bit.

So let them be on about their business. They're not suitable even as peasant stock. Their backs may be strong, but they are too weak in the heads.

I plan to replace them with a couple of shiploads of more suitable and sensible stock imported from the depths of the Congo.

So all in all, in two weeks time we shall see the Guy Estate being run on quite different lines.

Two weeks from now to pack up and ship out.

Don't bother to lock your door behind you.

Women Always Bawl

They had one of those women's rights commissioners on that open line radio programme Sunday night past. Tough as nails, tongue like a gimlet, face like a brass monkey. You could picture her from the way she talked. Full of wind and business, a piece of chain on her eyeglasses, blue rinse in her hair, as efficient and self-sufficient as some of those upalong professional women can be.

She got a number of calls, most of them from other women, that put a few shots across her bow. And then some really snarky broad from Montreal got on the line. She got in some very nasty digs.

After she hung up, the woman commissioner's voice started to wobble a bit and then for a minute or so she shut up altogether. It was obvious she was having a few sniffs for herself.

And there, to my mind, is the crux of the whole matter. Women bawl in public and men don't...outside of Frenchmen and Joe Namath and a few more. That is their nature. When it comes to the pinch, women always bawl.

A woman with the faucets turned on is an awesome thing. It takes the strength right out of your knees and leaves you without a word in your cheek. Now I don't mean these little tiffs they get into when they cry for spite or frustration.

But you take a woman bawling because she's really frightened or has been in receipt of some genuine lumps somewhere along the line and by the lard liftin', that has a most curious effect on you.

When we were in school at about ten or twelve years of age there was this fat girl whose family was not very well off. A lubberly and blundering sort of girl she was, with a certain snippishness and standoffishness to try and cover it up.

She came along one day wearing what looked like a new coat. Someone passed a remark about it and she made the mistake of making a snotty reply. Then the destruction began.

(By the way, there is no mystery why kids of a certain age all dress alike, look alike and talk alike. Or why some twelve-year-old will take the fits and vomit if not given a maxi or mini or whatever the rest of the gang happens to be wearing. Stark terror, that's all. She knows that if she's the slightest bit different she'll be picked apart. The recess ground and the hen's pen are much alike in this. If there's a hen with a feather out of place the rest will commence picking on it until they draw blood and then they will go into a frenzy.)

Anyway, we all started picking on the stunned fat girl with the new coat. We soon discovered that it wasn't a new garment at all, but an old one that her mother had remodelled for her and trimmed off with some ratty fur around the collar and cuffs. She really did look ridiculous in it.

But she had made the mistake of trying to be stuck up about it and, as I say, had responded in kind at that first snarky remark. The whole of recess time was devoted to the jolly sport of mocking and jeering her, with some of the boys even so bold as to catch hold of her and rip one of the pockets.

She disappeared just before the bell rang. On the way in I happened to pass by this seldom used porch and there she was, huddled in the corner under that piece of second-hand drygoods and tatty muskrat pelts.

As I passed by she glanced up and her face was red and swollen. I will never forget the look of misery and terror on her face. Even now when I happen to think of it, a certain shame and melancholy overtakes me.

Of course, things haven't been so dull along the line, thank heavens, that I have no more than that to blush at. But for some reason this particular incident remains especially vivid.

But there you have it. There's the difference between the two. Girls bawl at stuff like that, but boys don't. Even in those days I remember I used to put up a kick in the kitchen about having to wear certain garments...a serviceable pair of pants from the catalogue or a home-made sweater with bumblebee stripes or an oversized jacket from the parcel of second-hand clothes sent down from Montreal.

There was a chance you could stow it away in the sheep's house on the way to school and put in on again on the way home. But mostly you had to bear your cross.

Chaps did hear disparaging remarks about their clothes on the playground, but there was certainly no such thing as crawling into a corner and bawling about it. Lord save us, no. Chaps had two courses open to them.

At the first sign of being looked at askance on account of novel attire you could pick out one of the boys not too much bigger than yourself and commence to pound the sugar out of him. By the time the bell rang everyone was more interested in the fisticuffs, and garments on both sides had undergone considerable alterations anyhow.

Or, if you didn't feel up to scratch that day, you could start acting the fool and pass it off that way. You could stretch the homeknit sweather with the bumblebee stripes down around your knees and tear off around the playground giving an imitation of the Green Hornet or something.

But the poor brutes of girls had no other course open to them. Girls don't fight. Or if they do they look more comical and ridiculous than ever. Girls don't intentionally act the fool. In fact, you show me a woman with a real sense of humour and I'll show you a rare bird indeed.

They're trapped between the devil and the deep blue sea. Now you'll hear some women say that it would be better for men if they had the scattered bawl in public. This is nonsense. Big boys don't cry. Oh, they might have the odd blubber a couple of times a year, but no one is going to see them. It is not in their nature.

Meanwhile, a woman screeching has a curious effect on a man. If they were a bit smarter they'd spend less time fooling around with girdles and scent and spend more time on perfecting their ultimate weapon.

It is a difficult thing to fake and requires much practice. A chap can nearly always tell the difference between the real thing and the miserable little snivel put on for the sake of winning an argument or getting a new coat.

Some German bloke once said that all fondness, for want of a better term, is rooted in pity. He advised chaps to marry only ugly or deformed women. But that's going too far with it. Still, you must admit that the main inclination of men toward women (aside from a dislike of washing dirty socks) is caused by the need to have someone to protect.

This urge is born in men and is at least as strong as the natural fondness women have for their youngsters. Say, I wonder whatever happened to that stunned girl in the homemade coat? I dare say she made a good match and is happy as a lark.

Alas. And that spinster on the women's rights commission who had a genuine bawl on the radio Sunday night sounds a bit on the old side for me.

At this rate I'll have to either buy an automatic washer-dryer, or join Holy Orders.

Winter and the Outharbour Juvenile

A crucial difference between then and now is the distribution of heat into a house. Whereas these days heat gets upstairs as well as in the kitchen, in those times it went to robust extremes depending on where you were.

You had the tropics and the arctic within the confines of one dwelling. There was the kitchen with the Waterloo or Maid of Avalon stoked to the dampers, red enough to read fine print by, with an iron kettle and so many iron boilers heaving up steam by the wholesale, and there you had the Amazon jungle. Not a degree under ninety.

Come into the kitchen from outdoors on the hand of being frozen. Like the sauna baths we read about in other countries, the change greatly stirred the circulation, which is always good as regards hygiene.

On the other hand, if you rigged up for outdoors on a cold day you couldn't hang around the kitchen long once you had all your rigging on. You'd melt and run down in your boots.

The finest hour of the Waterloo stove was in the middle of a storm in the dead heart of the winter on the blackest night of the year with the wind a raging gale and the spray on the harbour sheet white and the frost bitter enough to crack the rocks and papers stuffed under the door to keep the draft out.

Then the only thing standing against the proceedings outside the window was the stove. The only thing, sir. It certainly got no help from the bit of clapboard and perhaps a bit of sawdust or goosegrass stuffed down between the chopped posts.

The bit of fire was all there was to stand against it. Give it a stir with the lifter, heave in a few more junks and see the flankers streaming away against the darkness.

But it was a different matter outside the kitchen. You might just as well bolt stark naked out the door into a ten-foot drift as go into the front room. Except that it was a little less windy.

No trouble to see your breath in the air in there, or your hand stick to the doorknob upstairs, or the frost on the bedroom windows devil-deep. A wonder the flame in the keorsene lamp didn't freeze.

Getting from the kitchen to the bed when the time came on a frosty night was a touchy business. First you had a drop of cocoa and a soda biscuit, then went out by the corner of the house, then came in and stood up by the stove to acquire as much heat as possible without scorching your garments. Then you made a bolt.

Off up the stairs with your beachrock in tow. It might sound sissy, but it was a matter of survival. A beachrock - or a brick in homes that could afford one - heated in the oven and put into two wool socks.

Sling the rock under the bedding, discharge your prayers with blasphemous haste, then scravel off your clothes down to the knitted undergarments.

Even by that length of time you were shivering almost too much to blow out the lamp, but you didn't need to because you could hold your hand over the top of the globe and snuff it out and not get burned.

Then the straight dive under the bedclothes, if you could find the bottom of it. About eighteen layers of bedclothes and, no doubt, not one too many. Once under you might as well be caught in a mine cave in.

The beds dragged down in the middle like hammocks and, with the heft of the clothes, you were hard pressed to draw one breath after the other.

By this time the frost on the window was thick enough to shut out the light of a full moon and the ice in the pot under the bed solid enough to bear up a small foreign car. By the time anti-freeze came along the modern conveniences were also available.

In the morning there was much the same drill except in reverse.

You had your choice of taking a chance of pulling on your clothes then and there or making a bolt for the kitchen with them under your arm.

All this, of course, is only a small part of winter as it affected the outharbour juvenile. Or the outharbour adult, for that matter. There were many other aspects to it, we know, both outside and in.

What effects it might have had in later years is a matter of opinion. But then, so is the effect on a juvenile of being reared in a house with the temperature in all parts at seventy degrees all year.

They're not likely to be so nimble on the stairs.

A Fortuitous Distillation

Your average Newfoundlander is waterproof, dustproof, shock resistant and anti-magnetic. Just as racehorses have been bred for legs and wind, he has been bred, over three or four hundred years, for durability. Your Newfoundlander will come out on top of it all. Endurance is his secret.

For centuries, back to the days of the first Elizabeth and our dread sovereign lord King James, the Newfoundlander has been taking his lumps and has learned a thing or two about hanging in there.

A long and determined assortment of harriers and exterminators, both native and imported, have struggled relentlessly through the years to rid the fair face of the world of this unlovely and irksome breed.

But there are some ugly weeds you can't root out of your pretty garden, misters, and there are some varmits you can't eradicate.

With the merry lash and the branding iron and the deportation ships they attacked this infestation of Newfoundlanders in the earliest days. With the torch and the wrecking bar they drove them to hide among two thousand holes in the rocks because they had no business to be here.

There to survive, alone amongst the fog forever, in suspicion of strange ships passing. Report the stranger at once, youngsters. It might be the pirates; it might be the French; or one of His Britannic Majesty's frigates dispatched to blast illegal settlers and their miserable heaps of sticks off the rocks.

This while the treasury of England built great mansions of stone in Virginia. All this while the ships of King Louis ferried loads of gold to establish massive citadels at Quebec and Louisbourg.

While they all sailed past to build enduring cities in Canada, the Newfoundlander was a squalid criminal not deserving the right to put a few damn sticks over his head for shelter.

While the solid colonial burghers cheered the governor's carriage as it passed through the streets of Williamsburgh and Quebec City, the Newfoundlander was kept in slavery and considered fit only to rip the guts out of codfish.

God save our gracious queen. Madam, my lady, may sometimes hear that there is still within her realms an inconsequential and barren Island whose citizens show a curious persistence to wave the Union Jack.

Let her not think – considering the treatment of Newfoundland by her ancestors – that she is being slyly mocked by this. The Present Sovereign is held in great esteem here because without her and all the kings and queens of England right back to the issue of Ann Boleyn, Newfoundlanders would today be mere Canadians or Americans.

Without the Star Chamber and the Fishing Admirals and the French Shore you wouldn't be able to tell the difference today between a Newfoundlander and a milk-fed Iowa farm boy. There'd be more blond hair and teeth per capita and instead of being peopled by gentle barbarians the place would be overrun by folks with guns.

Madam, my lady, and her whole ancestral gang were worthy adversaries and have earned our respect. Notice that while her soldiers dashed off across the plains to rescue her loyal Canadian subjects from the savages her sailors busied themselves burning her loyal Newfoundland subjects off the rocks. So she thoughtfully provided us with the most sport.

In the end, who's left? In the end there's the Heir Apparent and there's the manicured offspring of the citizens of Kingston and Halifax, and there's the durable issue of Newfoundland.

So you're a Lower Canadian? To rear you through the ages took a bit of wear and tear, too. The bleeding disease, the pox and the axe took a considerable toll of your crowd.

But for every death in the family it took to get you where you are today, any kid among the bushes in Newfoundland can claim a thousand sacrifices through starvation, overwork, disease, forced exile and persecution that went into the making of him.

Your Newfoundlander has undergone four centuries of an extremely rigorous breeding programme. Acts of God and Royal Warrants weeded out five or six of every ten born into the world alive. This fortuitous distillation has left us with an exceedingly durable race.

Who do you think is a better match for you, Charlie boy?

Or is there any contest at all?

Thinking Warm

February is not a bad time to be thinking warm.

Now, in the middle of it, when the snow is orange in the evenings and the humps in it make thin blue shadows. When the sun gives it up early for a bad job leaving a smear on the horizon as red as the lining of a sore throat.

Cold – a name for a miserable disease that is both common and incurable. Cold blue skies as opposed to warm blue which is the colour of ink on a letter you've read only three times so far.

Black trees in white snow. Evergreen? Nonsense. They're soot-black in the dead heart of winter, made so by the frost. Take notice.

Alders and birch as dead as barbed wire. Fit only for whips to lash an aching old horse when the iron runners grate on gravel patches. Fit only for baiting a snare of wire to strangle a rabbit while a black cloud muffles the moon.

All the cold we can bear. And there's March and cruddy April to go yet. This is a time for thinking warm.

I remember bits and pieces of Florida.

So hot that your eyebrows can't cope as you wait at stop lights on the streets of Tampa with all the windows down. The plastic car seats get soft and threaten to melt. Your brains simmer and bubble under your skull. Outside, the ultraviolet glare of the sun drains colour from everything and the noonday shadows are solid black.

Even on the beach, the dazzling white sand is too hot to touch and despite the wind the sweat runs in a steady stream down your spine. Turn over and your bellybutton fills up and overflows.

Hot wind pushes the breakers in over the shallow water. Walk on and on into the warm sea until you get tired and you're hardly to your middle. No cold blue here. Garish turquoise like a swimming pool lit from the bottom at night and green and purple streaks on the far horizon.

A tropical downpour when the water comes down in a solid piece and is halfway up the car wheels in five minutes. Even the rain is hot.

Out pops the sun again and the fish-belly white tourist is broiled and blistered in half an hour, a deep burn that can make you weak and nauseous and can even kill.

Around seven, winter and summer, the sun goes down suddenly and the night air is still as hot as the steam from the kettle. A hum starts in your head, a ringing in the ears, as if from a high fever.

It is an electronic whine that rises higher and higher like in the spy movies when they turn up the electricity on the poor beggar they're torturing.

Frogs the size of a thumbnail, hundreds of them in the trees all around, make the ringing in your head after dark. The heat goes on. Glump, glump, go the frogs in the swamps. Snakes and raccoons and God knows what else rustle in the bushes outside the tent.

Up pops the sun again, driving you out of the tent in less than fifteen minutes. Out into the hot water to cool off. Out into the shallow water of the reef to look down through a mask at the puffs and bladders and waving shreds and spines like steel knitting needles and black blobs like the brains of drowned pirates.

Inside the restaurants air conditioning wrestles the temperature down to seventy and you get the shock of stepping into an icebox. Out again and the smothering heat hits you in waves.

It is nearly dark in the camping park by the white sand and the green sea when a monstrous motorcycle roars up. A young man with a scarred face gets off, throws down a sleeping bag and, thunck, sticks a bayonet into the trunk of a palm tree.

The young couple from British Columbia in the campsite next to him exchange nervous glances. But he turns out to be a pleasant enough fellow to talk to.

125

Up through the mountains and across the gulf and east past the Hall's Bay Line where there's still snow on the hills and the rocky bones of Newfoundland stick through and the air is damp and chilly and immensely familiar.

Nice, in a miserable sort of way, to be back.

I Demonstrate My Inventive
Talents Once Again

On the third day of solitary confinement during the latest State of Emergency, I decided to throw myself into some project that would be to the benefit of mankind as a whole.

After much thought I settled on the improvement and refinement of an article which is in common use throughout Christendom; namely, false teeth. Civilization as we know it would be thereby improved and I would pass on in due course having made two blades of grass grow where only one had grown before.

As is the case in all these projects, the philosophy has to be well thought out. A little thought by a scientific mind will pinpoint the main fault of false teeth as they stand today.

They are not sharp enough. For they are made to look like natural teeth, yet far less jaw pressure can be applied to them. Consequently, the bite suffers and false teeth wearers, to their detriment, often end up with unchewed lumps of pizza pie bouncing around down in their guts.

Minutes passed into hours and hours into days as I studied the problem from every angle. It came to me in a flash as these things always do. I happened to glance down on the floor and my eye fell upon the sports pages of the weekend paper.

There, on page sixteen, was a likeness of a figureskater with the tools of her trade under her arm. And the blades of her skates were covered by a simple device, lengths of tough white plastic known as skate protectors.

"Eureka!" I cried, since it seemed to be the thing to do. Uppers and lowers consisting of stainless steel blades honed to the sharpness of a pair of scissors or a set of pinking shears. With a set of natural looking guards to slip on over them when the wearer got up from the table.

Imagine the vast improvement on tough steaks and corn cobs. Yet the concept was chastely simple – the efficient blades for eating, the natural looking protective caps for display, and that was it. With the addition perhaps of a small gap in front to allow for spitting out raspberry seeds.

Here we had a design that could be easily produced and put on the market in the price range well within the means of all classes. Simple, sturdy, efficient, cheap...the Volkswagen, as it were, of false teeth.

However, after a brief celebration, I did not stop there. All too often we inventors and innovators see our ideas taken up and exploited by others while we ourselves go down to paupers' graves.

So I applied myself to the task once more, this time looking for refinements and additions to the basic concept that would result in a deluxe product suited to the carriage trade.

The second came much easier than the first. The details are much too complicated to set down outside of a technical report, but the gist of it is that the sharper cutting or chewing edges are located immediately behind the normal-looking teeth...and may be raised or lowered at will!

Those who understand the working of airplane flaps or grader blades will grasp the idea at once. Through a system of gears, levers and counter-balances the cutting edges may be raised or lowered by means of a control lever which is located behind the left rear molar.

Tremendous versatility is offered by these deluxe dentures. The operator has only to insert a finger on the pretext of dislodging a shread of filet and select one of three forward gears plus overdrive.

First we have the "display" gear which might correspond to neutral or park on an automobile. With the lever in this position the working edges of the dentures are completely retracted behind the normal-looking facade.

Next we have what we might call "low gear". In this position the cutters are lowered a mere tenth of an inch for light work such as chewing gun, biting fingernails, or nipping off thread.

Then we have "utility gear", the most versatile of all. With the shift lever in this position the working edges are extended a quarter of an inch for snacks, treats and general eating. Friends will be amazed at the rapidity which which you can now whip through the toughest pot roast and will marvel at the neat no-nonsense bite marks in your toast, your apples and your slices of raw bologna.

Finally, we come to "overdrive". Here you have the option of really "opening her out" as the saying goes. This is a gear designed with an eye to the times in which we live.

It extends your stainless steel gnashers a full half inch, both uppers and lowers, and is designed with anti-aggression potentiality in mind. In a word, defence.

Thus equipped you are at last in a position to teach that saucy dog on your block a lesson which he so richly deserves. And you may have no fear of walking to work through dark culprit-infested alley-ways.

Even before you have time to give the police sergeant the particulars of the incident the constable will enter with the culprit in tow:

"We picked up the culprit wot accosted this gentleman, sergeant. Found him down in the vicinity of Beck's Cove bleedin' to death. Minus, funnily enough, 'is nose and 'is left thumb. Odd case, this."

Needless to say, there are a few drawbacks to this vastly improved masticating machinery, but nothing that can't be overcome. If, for instance (and not to be indelicate about it), the wearer should be involved in a spot of passionate earlobe nibbling and accidentally shift to overdrive in the heat of the moment, the result could be unfortunate indeed. But a word to the wise should be sufficient.

Now, I see that at last the snowplow is advancing up the road, and I must gather up my blueprints and specifications and bring them down to lay before the medical faculty of the university. The few paltry millions I get from the patents will all be plowed back into my researches, need I add.

Some people may ask why I did not turn my inventive talents to other fields. Perhaps if I had I could have come up with a painless cure without surgery for protruding cabinet ministers, for instance.

I can only reply that it all depends on circumstances. Had I been stormbound at the Golden Eagle restaurant near the Holyrood intersection with the Premier yesterday, the story might have been different.

St. Patrick's Day

So far as celebration is concerned, St. Patrick's comes at a right time of year. It provides a small break in the austere season of Lent and coincides with our first glimpse of the end of a long hard winter.

In fact, there is a saying in this country that on March 17 "Paddy takes the cold stone out of the water" and the first snow flurry after St. Patrick's Day is known as "Sheila's Brush."

This year, our people whose ancestors came from Ireland must look back to the country of their fathers with considerable sorrow and emotion.

"Troubled Ulster" has been in the news all year and is one of the most barbarous and shocking things on the world scene today. I should imagine that many here are inclined to "take sides" from a distance. Especially those who have come from there to Newfoundland in the past few years.

Just as those Newfoundlanders of English extraction were affected to see their antecedent country involved in such a sorry debacle as Suez, so must "Troubled Ulster" affect some of us strongly now.

But let us remember that our country is neither England nor Ireland nor even Scotland. It is Newfoundland. Without being parochial or narrow, we should be able to view events in other countries more objectively and with cooler heads.

In recent years we have seen younger Americans come into Newfoundland bringing with them the bitterness and frustration of that troubled country.

While, as citizens of the world, we must be concerned with the troubles of the world, we do still have an advantage in our geographical isolation.

Newfoundland is still, in that sense, a retreat - a place still removed from the blood and smoke where, in relative calm and safety, perhaps some small bits of civilization may be kept alive.

In ages past, the Irish saved a precious thing when the world was afire and they retreated and clung to the rocks at Iona.

There is a small island by that name in Newfoundland.

Not This One; The First One

"Cock your pistols, Charlie,

"The French is comin' now!"

That used to be the favourite song of a person belonging to our place in a certain Far Greater Bay.

It was not in my lifetime, but the older people out there, every now and then, will say, "Cock your pistols, Charlie!" and add that that was poor old uncle so-and-so's favourite song which he used to sing at dances.

If you think I am telling lies about this then, sir, you are no better than you ought to be! You can ask any of the older race out there about it and they will tell you the same thing.

It is another reminder that Newfoundland had been in operation long before that infamous April Fool's Day in 1949.

Another person belonging to that place was also up to date on war songs. During the First World War he used to sing the first two lines of his favourite:

"Cheer, boys, cheer! Sebastapol is taken!

"Cheer, boys, cheer! The enemy is shaken!"

Then he would stop and sigh wistfully that..."Er, there don't seem to be no good songs comin' out of this war like there was out of the last."

So World War One was a dead loss as far as he was concerned.

When I was a child they had a hard job trying to break me of saying "winder" instead of "window".

After being chastised I would go on about my business and recall what Uncle Phil said to Aunt Sarah.

He happened to remark one day that there was "a wonderful sight of hern out there this morning."

"Hern!" said Aunt Sarah. "Hern! Tut, tut, tut. That's no way to say it. You should say herring."

"Alright, then," said Uncle Phil, "HAIR-ing, ye bloody scholar!"

Although an oldish country, we have little to show for it in the way of ruined castles, old papers and books. But one of our relics – though little noticed – is that we are still in possession of bits of the Queen's English.

Our Sovereign Lady, Queen Elizabeth's. Not this one; the first one.

She used to refer to these little insects which run up your rubbers on the berry hills as "emmets" and there are many among the younger race in Newfoundland today who think it odd to call them "ants".

Our Lady, Gloriana, a First Class Curser, used to shout "Zounds!" in times of stress which is short for "God's wounds!", or scream "God's blood!" at sweet Sir Walter.

A person tells me that at his place – in a lesser though substantial bay – some people are still in the fashion of saying "Godzooks!" when things get out of kilter.

What's that short for? "God's socks"? But we see in the old English books that they used to go about saying "Godzooks!" morning, noon and night.

Dad – when someone gets a good one over on him – says: "You cod of misery! Deuce hoist you, anyway!"

Of course, when things get hotter he puts it a touch stronger than that.

But we see by the books that "Deuce" is quite an old name for the Devil. So there's another one handed down to us from olden days. And what do we make of "Says I, the devil haul ye and your Kelligrews Soiree?"

Perhaps it was originally "the devil have all of ye" or something of that nature. It must be a great pastime looking for the roots of all these things.

The "Godzooks!" person and myself once wrote down in an

exercise book some of the words and sayings from our respective bays.

On looking back over it, the things that strike you is how much of what some might call "coarse language" there is in it.

But there is a reason for this. In the old days people weren't so nice in themselves as they are now. In between there somewhere - perhaps in the days of the Old Queen - they started getting refined and genteel.

They found or made up "respectable" words to replace the common name for some things which had been in use since Adam. They also made skirts to cover up the shameful legs - excuse me, "limbs" - of their pianos.

Furthermore, for some reason, a word or expression which sounds funny when spoken looks vulgar when put into print.

So you can only beat around the bush. Thus, if you wanted to say how they might describe how thick the fog is in Placentia Bay you have to say "Thick as a gallon of (excrement deleted) in a quart jug."

Being under such a hindrance when writing on a subject of this sort, I expect I will have to go on about my business and leave it at that.

If of a suspicious nature you may say, "Ah ha, he has found still another excuse for shirking and not putting out all he has got so as to finish up early and get a little longer weekend out of it."

"You cod of misery," I say. "Deuce hoist you, anyway!"

135

The Quick and the Dead

You'll never learn anything if you don't get out around and mingle with the people and take notice of what is what.

The weather being somewhat clement yesterday, I got into my motorcar and took a turn around the western side of one of our larger bays. My wanderings took me to the shores of picturesque Boarding House Reach on which is located the thriving community of Little Nasty Cove East.

This settlement is typical for its size in Newfoundland, having fourteen dwelling houses, six grocery stores and three denominational schools. It was half past two when I motored through the city gates but there was no sign of life.

There were no people on the roads and, apart from three horses lounging around the post office yard, it seemed deader than a Liberal Leadership Convention.

I was about to turn around and go away again when I heard the sound of a dull explosion coming from the direction of the graveyard. So I left my conveyance and proceeded toward the cemetery on foot.

There were two men in the middle of the enclosure which was about as big as a descent-sized cabbage garden and fenced around with white palings.

"Good day, men, good day," I said. "What's the work today?"

"Oh, a bit of this and a bit of that, sir," said one of them, pausing to lean on his shovel. "Er, before you comes through that gate, sir, I must ask you a bold question. Have you got either transmittin' or receivin' radio device anywhere on your person?"

"No, indeed, my good man," I replied. "None whatsoever."

"Good enough then, sir," he said. "There's blasting going on here you know and you can't be too careful so far forth as what dynamite is concerned, can you?"

I agreed that this was very much the case and then I made myself known to the two labourers. They then introduced themselves to me as Messers Leviticus Thompson and Balthazar Parsons, life-long residents of Little Nasty Cove East.

They seemed pleasant enough chaps to talk to, so I passed a remark on the apparent absence of life in the community itself as compared to the unusual amount of it here in the graveyard.

"Winter Works Programme, sir," explained Leviticus. "The entire work force of Little Nasty Cove East - me and he - is employed here under a federal grant from Ottawa."

"The youngsters is all in school, the short term and long term assistance crowd is gone down to Spigot Harbour to change their cheques and the women and pensioners is all in out of the cold."

"If you're putting together a piece on this for the paper I expect you'll be wanting to draw us out. Balt here is the man for that. He got the education. I'm only a fisherman myself, although I didn't get enough stamps last year."

Balthazar informed me that his trade was, in a manner of speaking, going to trade school. He said he had been at it for six years running, got his Grade 10 at upgrading school and was so far a qualified ship's cook, bricklayer, diesel repairman, barber and plumber's helper.

"It pays fairly well but I struck a slack season so I signed up with winter works for a change. We got this grant through the clergy here. They got together and send me and he in to Sin John's as a committee. We ast the feller in the Sir Humphries Gilbert Building what...."

"Er, excuse me for telling you, sir, but you're treading on poor old Mr. Thompson, this man here's great great grandfather. We must have respect for the dead, mustn't we sir, the poor old buggers."

"Yes, we ast the feller in back of the counter what they had for us and he said the most popular winter works projects in

Newfoundland was building recreation fields and fixin' up graveyards. He said Otterwa was taking care of both the quick and the dead.

"So we ast him what this recreation fields was and he said sport. Now we didn't think much of that. We all likes our little bit of sport now and then, but we'd sooner go at it upstairs undercover than out in the fields. Besides, the clergy wouldn't hold with it.

"So we said we would take fixin' up graveyards and he said he thought that was a pretty good choice and a cut above breaking rocks anyway. So Little Nasty Cove East was put down for an $83,000 fixin' up graveyards grant and here we are."

I was much heartened to find that native enterprise and initiative is still very much alive in this Country and I asked the two persons if they would be so good as to take me on a tour of the project.

It was revealed to me that there were approximately thirty-five persons interred here in Little Nasty Cove East necropolis, although it was hard to say as not all the resting places had been marked.

The winter works project had started three weeks ago and was, so far, on schedule despite several heavy snowfalls on the site. A good fence had been put around it two years ago so no new work was called for there.

"We have been grubbing the gowithy off poor old Uncle Tom Cromwell for the past five days and now we're starting at beautifyin' the rest of the grounds. The plans call for a dog rose apiece on all the old gentlemen, columbines on the old ladies, a bleeding heart for the infants and a nice border of mussel shells on them what was lost at sea.

"So pretty a picture as ever you'd wish to see, sir, when the summer comes. A pleasure to be lowered down here, it will. Down that end we're digging a half dozen holes ready for new customers, although no one crossed over in this place for ten years past.

"Aunt Molly Pritchett, they says she's a hundred and seven year old although I never seen her birth certificate myself. But she took wonderful bad on Old Christmas Day and have been on the hitch ever since."

I enquired as to what chance of survival they thought a transplanted clump of columbines had in Newfoundland in the middle of February but they said that that end of it was out of their jurisdiction altogether.

"That's Otterwa's look out, now isn't it, sir. Winter works projects got to be done in the winter and that's the law. Now, then, all stand back and take cover. We're going to fire another shot."

They placed an overly large quantity of dynamite on the ground, packed it down with snow and lit the fuse. The frozen earth erupted in a small crater and a roundish object the size of an enamel dipper flew through the air and pitched in a snowbank.

"By God, Levi, look-a-here! The relics of your poor great great grandfather. Not much of a family resemblance I must say. Certainly, they was only stout on your mother's side. Of course, they had it hard back in them days. Little or nothing to eat. Well, we'll lodge the old gentleman back in the hole. Just the size for a nice hardy dog rose, what? Got the time on you, sir? Bless my soul, twenty a'past three. Hard work never hurt no one but no need to go to hell with it I always says. I think we'll cut her off right here and come back tomorrow."

My sentiments exactly.

Footwear as Regards the Outharbour Juvenile

It is nothing less than surprising the extent to which footwear loomed large in the life of a juvenile of our outharbours in times gone by.

Good ankle support was greatly stressed in the early years. From the time an infant was able to toddle he was laced into what was called "a good sturdy boot" for the sake of ankle support.

By the age of five or six, he was wearing such sturdy boots affording unexcelled ankle support that if knocked out by, say, a beach rock thrown by a companion, he would not topple over but merely flip forward from the waist.

Indeed, many outharbour juveniles reared strictly according to the principles of good ankle support and a sturdy boot often fell flat on their faces the first time they put on shoes. They had two extra joints down there they had never used before.

Shoes were not much favoured even in later years for the simple fact that they were useless except for hard snow. It was impossible to walk one hundred feet in any direction without sinking past the insteps into one viscous substance or another.

Lumps were almost as bad. These items were apparently hacked out of solid blocks of gutta'percha rubber with little eye to the differences in foot size or the shape of the right foot as compared to the left.

The main virtue of lumps is that they "stood up", which is to say that even the most ambitious and active outharbour juvenile could not hope to wear out his lumps inside of five years.

On the other end of the scale from lumps were long rubbers. Business executives may have their jet planes, but the outharbour juvenile knew the supreme thrill of being presented with his first pair of long rubbers.

There is a certain buccaneer swash to long rubbers whether they are folded down once allowing the white linings to show in a rakish fashion or folded up again with the straps flicking nicely and the buckles jingling at every step.

There is always the job of testing them during the first several weeks of wear. The testing of a long rubber involves seeing how far you can walk out into the water without going over the top.

Since there is absolutely no way to tell what the extreme limits are without going beyond them and backing up, a proper test of a long rubber entails getting it full of water. For how do we know what is enough until we have had too much?

Another piece of footwear much favoured by the outharbour juvenile was the logan which consists, essentially, of two refined rubber lumps attached to knee-length leather uppers.

They are secured by means of great yellow laces, six feet or more in length, which are crisscrossed through numerous eye-holes and then hitched back and forth through rows of hooks near the top. With a set of new laces your logan boot cut nearly as much dash as your long rubber.

A favourite of the author was always the knee rubber. Here, to his mind, is an item of footwear ideally suited, except for the depths of summer, to year round use in the outharbour.

While not so jaunty as the long rubber, it is far better suited, with two pairs of stockings inside, to the slushy footing of winter than is the logan. It affords more protection from seepage whilst traversing both beach and bog, and is less heavy than the long rubber.

The knee rubber - of "Hood", "Blue Bar" or "Miner" manufacture - was a constant piece of equipage in the winter's wardrobe from earliest days onward.

As for the depths of summer, which in hardier times extended from the middle of May to the middle of October, the sneaker boot was the only item of footwear into which the outharbour juvenile would suffer himself to be forced without a struggle.

The new feminist discarding her foundation garments by way of protest scarce knows the great feeling of liberation experienced by the outharbour juvenile transferring from the long or knee rubber to the sneaker boot for the summer. Having dropped some twenty pounds of weight he could easily up his top speed by fifteen miles per hour.

Curiously enough, the favourite summer footwear among many juveniles was no footwear at all. With two weeks practice, your average outharbour juvenile was able to maintain a steady trot, barefoot, along the gravel road.

And this to the startled profanity of older folk, such as "Good Glory!" or "Blessed Fortune!" Bloodpoisoning was greatly feared should the juvenile tread on a nail or piece of glass. However, the boots came off on every possible occasion.

I don't recall anyone being struck down by bloodpoisoning.

Tea and Sympathy

"Gotcha!" whooped the little old lady as she plunged the point of her umbrella about two feet into the old navel.

Before I could recover she had brought her handbag up in a vicious arc and connected with the right earhole which felled me like a polled ox on the sidewalk in front of my place of employment.

"Malicious weakener of the democratic process!" she shrieked, while fetching me a flurry of kicks to the shortribs with the toe of her gaiter.

"Outrageous, unjustified attacker of the government!" she screeched, bringing the brolly into action again in a wicked series of jabs below the belt. "Servile minion of the Baron of Fleet! Irresponsible denizen of that cesspool of cynics!"

She had taken me unbeknownst. I had barely caught the glimpse of her fox fur neckpiece and the next thing I knew I was flat out on terra firma counting the stars at midday.

"Cheapest form of yellow journalist!" she cried, attempting to mash my head flat with her handbag. "Poison pen anarchist! No good to try and hide under that cowardly cloak of innuendo and implication now!"

"Really, madam!" I managed to gasp. "This cowardly cloak of innuendo and implication as you call it cost me $29.95 on sale at

143

the Big Seven and if you do not desist at once I shall be sending you round the dry cleaning bill for it!"

"None of your lip, you misleader and damager of the province!" whooped the old dear, getting a fresh wind. "I'm going to trounce that pure political bias and disgusting malicious garbage right smacksmooth out of you."

She got in a few more telling licks before tottering backwards against a parking meter, one hand to her bosom, looking slightly peaked.

"Don't stir! Stay right where you is," she panted while fishing a crock of large brown and purple tablets out of her purse, "because you got a lot more comin' to you yet."

Had she not got one of her nasty pills caught in her wind pipes I expect I would have been laid off starkers by now with the old tag on the big toe.

But the poor dear commenced to cough alarmingly and I picked my tattered form up out of the municipal gutters and went to her assistance.

"I expect you'll be wanting a soft drink to flush that pellet of physic clear of the tonsils, madam," I said. "If you will step inside I believe that can be arranged.

She seized the cannister of beverage from the drink machine and took it down like a Foreign Legion camel that had been ridden hard for a fortnight. It did the trick and she sat down to let her pill do her good.

"If it hadn't been so handy to pension day," she said in a slightly more composed frame, "I'd have sooner slipped me wind on the spot than step inside the door of this malicious cesspool of screwball cynics and poison pens!"

The reason for her umbrage began to dawn on me. The barmy old battleaxe had taken recent endearments from the government quarters about the daily paper to heart. Well, the New Regime could hardly wish for a more wiry vessel of wrath.

"Where do you crowd get the gall," she croaked with such renewed spirit that I took the precaution of arming myself with a loose bannister from the stairway, "to stick your faces in public after saying all them nasty malicious things about poor Mr. Smallwood?

"Don't deny it!" she crowed like a Leghorn rooster in heat. "Don't deny it because I heard it all on the radio this morning. The premier said you was nothing but a bunch of cause-clamoring negative axe-grinders.

"He always said you was a nest of dirty Tories and he finally run out of patience with you, eh? He says the public got to be protected against you lot, and I'm just the girl to do it!"

She had brought her brolly up into the en garde position again and skipped nimbly about like Manolete eager for the tail and both ears.

I saw no other course but to distract her attention momentarily by means of a clever subterfuge and tipped her head over heels into a large container of waste paper.

"Now then, my dear women," I said as she cut and thrust ineffectually from her confining position. "It seems that you are clearly behind the times. Do forgive me for pointing it out, but poor Mr. Smallwood is no longer among us.

"I suppose that a long-time devotee of that political gentleman may find his departure hard to accept, but really, madam, we must face facts.

"When you now hear a reference to "the premier" on the radio it is not poor Mr. Smallwood but his successor to whom they refer," I continued in a patient and Christian manner.

"In fact, though I hesitate to break the news, he has been replaced by a new regime of dirty Tories. There, there, madam, contain yourself or I fear you will injure your health further."

"Story-teller!" she shrieked, with a murderous lunge that nearly upset the wastepaper bin. "If the dirty Tories have took over from poor Mr. Smallwood, then how come they're attacking you nest of dirty Tories here at the newspaper office?"

"I'm afraid I'm not qualified to answer that, ma'm," I said, ripping a piece off my tattered cloak of cowardly innuendo and implication with which to staunch a rather nasty scalp laceration.

"It is a metaphysical question best put to your priest, rabbi, parson or minister but not after he has a hard day in the pulpit. Us laymen should never dabble in either the divine mysteries or Newfoundland politics."

"Oh, my poor head," sighed the dear soul, the steam now gone entirely out of her. "It is too much for me to take in. God be with the good old days when life was simple and you knew where you stood."

"Yes," I said, helping her out of the trash bale and adjusting her fox fur about her doughty dewlaps. "As has been said we are indeed in the throes of 'future-shock' when yesterday's nest of dirty Tories suddenly becomes today's critics of the PC government and thus the weakeners of the democratic process.

"Adjustment must be especially hard for an ardent fan of poor Mr. Smallwood such as yourself," I said. "For you are hard-pressed to know whether to side with us nest of dirty Tories here at the newspaper or that nest of dirty Tories at Confederation Building."

She took a bottle of Minard's Linament out of her handbag and applied it to her nostrils.

"Never you mind, my dear woman," I said, giving her an encouraging pat on the tail of her fox. "Today's fast-paced society takes its toll of us all. We hear on the radio today that Mr. Moores has taken to his bed under the strain of it."

The news seemed to cheer her up somewhat and I accepted a kind invitation to drive her home in my motor car and went in for a nice cup of tea.

As soon as her next pension cheque arrives she plans to take out a subscription in an effort to keep up with the times.

Good Friday in the Outharbour

The only right and proper occupation for the Outharbour Juvenile on Good Fridays was Getting Mussels. Shortly after 3 p.m. you saw a small congregation of juveniles heading off along shore. They limped slightly for they had just been on their knees for the better part of three hours.

This had mangled the juvenile kneecaps and pretty well suspended the juvenile circulation below the waist. Faith of our fathers living still, in spite of dungeon, fire and strife and all that. Good Friday was no barrel of laughs, I can tell you.

For a start, you had nothing to eat that day except a bit of pickled herring and a boiled potato. You could hear the solemn belches all over the church. But the most wear and tear was occasioned by the special sacred music appropriate to the day.

This was a composition entitled "The Story of the Cross" which was printed up on a special four-page pamphlet and contained umpteen and ten verses and the instruction "To be sung with the priest, clergy, chaplains, vergers and all the people kneeling."

It was not what you might call a rollicking air even when you consider the day it was. It wasn't something they tended to rattle through. By the fourteenth verse you sought to ease your crunching kneecaps by resting your tailbone on the edge of the seat and slouching.

A sharp nudge in the ribs soon brought the juvenile back to a more pious position. For two or three reasons this epic hymn was what they called "dragged out nice and slow" far beyond the limits of solemnity.

Most of the women had new perms for one thing. Home permanents. The Prom or the Toni, a new innovation. It must have been forceful stuff because it smelled like a sickroom disinfectant and for the first week or so their hair was kinked up like those Afro hairdos so-called.

The perms were intended for the Easter socials but they had to put them in a week beforehand so they could get them combed out again into some semblance of nature in time for the Resurrection.

But by Good Friday they were already looking pretty swanky. Nothing, except a new hat, fosters piety in church so much as a new perm. And nothing is such an outward and visible sign of an inward and spiritual grace as extremely slow hymn-singing.

If the three Marys had been wearing new hats from Sear's catalogue they would have been looking more holy, if possible, than they do in their pictures.

Anyway, the women with the new perms tended to keep the hand brake on the singing. Another reason for the slowdown was the fact that a contingent from the Army was present. The Salvation Army.

They always came to church on Good Friday but on Easter Sunday a good many of the church people went to the Army. They were better at the Hallelujas. Even on ordinary days the singing slowed down considerably whenever there was a detachment from the Army present.

The Army people were louder singers and more spirited as is their custom. At first they would try to slow down to the doleful cadences of the Established Church but then they would get carried away and step it up a bit.

So the Church crowd, to show that there was none of that frivolity and handclapping around here, brother, had to rise their volume and slow the tempo down even more to keep them in their place.

All in all, by the time they got to the twenty-second verse, the rendition had ground down to a sort of arthritic groan such as you get when you hold your finger against the rim of a phonograph record. It was inspiringly drear to an extreme.

Even the nearing prospect of sugar in the tea and tobacco in the pipe after forty days and forty nights of going without did little to spoil the heroically holy disposition of those assembled.

At last, after the longest aaaaaaawwwwwwmmeennn of the whole year (sixteen seconds according to the author's Hopalong Cassidy wristwatch) it was over and all hands crippled out the door.

After changing back into civilian clothes, many of the juveniles met together, drawn by some mysterious force and set off on that peculiar outharbour delight, "Getting Mussels."

It was, of course, indulged in at other times of the year, but on nothing like the scale of Good Friday's expedition. It had to do with the tides. The water fell lower than it did at any other time, the beaches became twice as broad and rocks away out were breaking water.

"Now don't you go gettin' your feet wet. Mind now." This was the standard marching orders the juvenile got whenever he went out the door and the only ones.

Get your arms wet. Get your back wet. Stick your head under water for twenty minutes. But don't dampen those precious lumps down there attached to your ankles. You got a long way to walk yet.

Needless to say, the outharbour juvenile always got his feet wet, and they were never wetter than when he was Getting Mussels. The occupation called for wet feet. More often than not it entailed getting wet all over.

Since the North Atlantic, even in our southern bays, is none too toasty at that time of year, the delightful aspects of getting mussels may not be readily apparent.

But after the ordeal of Good Friday devotions, firewalking or being bottom man on a pit saw would have been downright jolly.

Live and Let Die
Thoughts for an Easter Sunday

An extra nice ham, glazed and dressed with raisin sauce, is the usual centerpiece for the Easter dinner these days.

Or some people prefer a roast leg of lamb relished with mint and served up with mashed potatoes and gravy.

And the children gorge themselves on huge candy eggs of chocolate and marshmallow brought to them by the Easter Bunny.

Yet the first of eight million people expected to starve in Africa before the year is out have been found dead, their stomachs filled with earth which they were driven to eat.

Ignorance is no excuse now.

We are in full knowledge of the fact that over half the people in this world are either undernourished or starving.

Communications have made the world so small that there is no more excuse for our ignoring the millions of people starving to death in Africa and Asia than if the family next door was suffering starvation.

Yet we look around and manufacture excuses to cover our consciences.

But excuses won't let us off the hook and the hook is this: by what right under the sun does one half of the population of the world live amid waste and gluttony while the other half endures the pangs of starvation?

If the world belongs to all, and all are equal in the sight of God, then where does the present situation fit in?

From time to time the rising cost of living in Canada is headlined. So times are "hard" for us these days. But we are the worst kind of hypocrites if we try to say we are poor off on only two or three meals of meat a week compared to others in the world who would fight to the death for the hind leg of a rat.

We in the rich part of the world have more than one hundred times our share of the world's goods.

We know all these things. The eight million who will die of starvation this year are forerunners of the twenty, forty, or eighty million who will die in a few years to come.

This half, so rich that not to be able to eat beefsteaks every other day is considered a "hardship," cries out that every little shortage is a crisis, while people in other parts of the world gnaw at the very ground in their last agonies.

Easter Sunday is the one day of the year when the churches are generally filled. Some people go along to show off their new clothes and some out of habit and some because they are religious.

What great Christians we all are. If the value of the church buildings we sit in had been put instead to sensible charity, countless millions would not be dying in agony today.

Small wonder the churches in later times have either played down or done away with the notion of hell altogether.

The prospects of hell combined with the magnitude of the sin being committed by us daily against our brothers in the other half of the world would, if preached strongly enough from the pulpits, drive congregations away from the church in stark terror.

We wish to be left comfortable. We don't want the few rotten and flimsy bandages we have wrapped around our consciences to be stripped away. We want to hang on to the attitude of "every man for himself and God for us all."

Of course, there have always been starving people around in the world, and always indifference to their plight.

But now they are dying in such vast numbers while those responsible for their deaths are fully informed of the situation, it is hard to see how churchfulls of burping people being cheerful at Easter is not more devilish than it is anything else.

It is a great blasphemy and spittle on the face of God.

What A Charm, What A Racket

Let us turn now to the quiet nostalgia of simpler times, and read from "Guy's Encyclopedia of Juvenile Outharbour Delights." We open to the entry on "Music in the Juvenile Sinner's Ears."

This has to do with the various sounds open to the outharbour juvenile. Or, rather, which used to be open to him.

There used to be loud bangs in the night then. Well, less like a bang and more like a loud "pong". I always thought, until recently, that they were caused by the bigger boys out late on the roads firing rocks down at the fishermen's empty Acto casks on the stagehead.

But these later years I found out that the heat from the sun used to make the barrels puff up in the daytime and in the nights when they cooled off they'd make a loud "pong".

You could hear all this going on from up in the bunk. You could hear all sorts of transactions. I always had the fashion of sleeping with my head as handy to the window as possible.

Calm nights when it was foggy and the window was up a bit and there was hardly enough breeze to knock the curtain scrim about, you could hear the long, slow grind of the tide on the beaches very far away.

You could hear a tin can bonking against the strouters on the rocks down there in the landwash, and you could hear the scattered peep of a cocksparrow almost too groggy to keep his eyes open.

First thing you could hear in the mornings was a few woody sort of klunks and the punt oars where the fishermen were shoving off to their collars.

Then you would hear the splashing where they were bailing her out with the piggin if it had rained the night before, and then you would hear a few "pffttts" from the priming cup, a few backfires and then "chunck-chunck-chunck" right out through the harbour.

Some people say it is "buck-buck-buck-buck" but I think that would be more like your Atlantic than your average Acadia.

At that hour of the morning you didn't hear them talking to each other very much. Finally, when the whole chorus of motorboats had started up and faded away out the harbour you would hear a rooster crowing somewhere over across the mesh.

Houses in those days, although a bit airish, were wonderfully suited to hearing what was going on out of doors.

It might be worth anyone's while even in this day and age to have one bedchamber that is not stuffed and stogged up with insulation and double pane glass.

You could hear every pat of the rain on the roof, every howl and whistle and squeak when it blew, you knew exactly what transactions were going on out doors without getting out of bed.

Apart from that, the frost which forms on the single-glass windowpane is quite interesting to the juvenile. All the trees and ferns and stuff. When they're frosted right up you can either blow a hole in them with your breath to see out, or you can lodge your tongue on them – if you want it peeled. Or you can make the print of your hand.

When the juvenile was laid up in bed with the measles and so forth he could hear a slow "chuff, chuff, chuff" noise in his head and a distant ringing like somebody frying in a frying pan.

On windy nights there was always a bottle howling somewhere – that is to say, the wind blowing across the neck of the bottle. Never failed. Always the neck of an empty bottle cocked up to the wind whichever way it blew.

Even when all the rest of the racket stopped, you could always hear a peculiar and very small "click, click, click" from somewhere down around the baseboards. Some people called it the deathwatch.

Say about the middle of February when the lambs came along,

the sheep used to kick up the hell of a racket in the evenings, sunny evenings, when people brought them up some scraps and hauled down a bit of hay to them.

This Russian person, Chagall, paints pictures of sheep just the spitting image of those ones, as I have discovered in my later years.

In the winter, in the woods, coming down the slide paths you would hear the bells jingling on the horses to give anyone coming along the path against them a chance to find a good place to haul off to one side.

Or you could hear the screech of the slide runners when they hit a patch of gravel and, if it was dark enough, see the sparks fly off.

Horses tackled up in the summer used not to be all the time bolting about like the ones we see in the western motion pictures. You could hardly hear them put their hocks down for the scrunching of the box cart wheels or the long cart wheels on the gravel.

One funny thing about sounds had to do with the school bell. In September it started off so merry. But by the time June came it sounded like the most dreariest thing in the world. We used to think that the clapper in it was getting sick and tired of being beat around.

The best time the church bell sounded was when it came from a long distance and you got a glimpse of it when the wind baffled.

When there was a funeral they would toll it slow and it was just like one hell of a big water tap with a very slow drip of holy water. Even when there was a gale of wind the church bell tolling for a funeral made it sound dead calm.

If you were going to have weather it was no trouble to hear the railway train blowing and that three mile away. When you were really going to have weather you could even hear the engines.

Nearly every outharbour mother has got the lungs of one of them opera singers. They could split your ears if you happened to be standing alongside of them and they were singing out to their own youngsters to come down and go up to the shop for them.

In the evenings they all got going at the one time singing out to their youngsters wherever they were to come in and get their suppers. Talk about making the valley ring! No need for loud speakers in those days.

Hearing people sawing off wood was as common as dirt, of course, upon what they called their "chipyard" and you could also hear them cleaving it up and the axe strike and them rending the junks apart with their hands and chucking it into the pile.

Hens were comical in the mornings when you went up to look in the hen's house. They'd be all hunched down on the nest looking sour as the cats, trying to get their eggs along and sputtering and grumbling to themselves.

What they said was, "Quarrk, quarrrk. Puck-puck-puck, puck — AARRRFFFF!" But us wicked little boys, though laced to Sunday School regular, used to say that what they were saying was someting else! These days that is nothing at all.

You would hear the weather birds in the spring in the evenings when you were up playing rounders, and what birds they seemed to be who could fly so high no one could see them but make so loud a noise that everyone could hear them.

I didn't like it at all when someone told me that it was only the bloody snipes diving down through the air and making the noise with their wings. What is the need of telling people old stuff like that?

I saw it explained the other day why there was a sound when there was no sound at all. A person was giving a talk on radio and said that some people's ears, when they are only youngsters, can even hear the molecules of air striking against their eardrums.

Certainly, lots of other people must have had that experience, too. It is an odd sound. It is not the same as when you are laid up in bed with the chicken pox, but sounds much more good like it is the sound the whole world is making.

But it is still a mystery why everything seemed to the outharbour juvenile – with all this dreadful charm and racket constantly going on – why everything then seemed so quiet, so damned quite, for all that.

Every Man Must Do His Bit

The Governor has been ordered off to Bermuda for a month for the good of his health.

Please God, a sojourn in a less barbaric climate will do His Honour worlds of good. Like the rest of us, he has been under shot and shell since last November.

There wasn't much we didn't get in the shapes of weather during the past six months clear of showers of frogs and a tornado or two.

The gods are angry. There's too much coarse language being used in Newfoundland. Libertinism. Avarice, malice, envy and unpleasantness of that nature. Not to mention those discount Co-op gas pumps.

We are getting the lumps we jolly well deserve. Before it's all over I expect there'll be more than the Governor will have to take off on rest and recreation leave.

Not to be an alarmist about it, but at this rate we could be getting our twelve inches of blizzard a night right up until the middle of July. And after that a deluge of congealed night soil.

In fact, we may have placed our finger on the crux of the matter right there. Everything from A-bombs to moon landings to an abundance of dogberries has been blamed for our worsening weather.

But most scientists agree now that it is largely caused by the unmannerly and unhygienic practice of airplanes flushing their toilets while in flight. When the forecast tells us that a storm "dumped six inches of snow" on central Newfoundland it is only half right.

According to studies conducted at Cornell University, the practice of flushing airplane toilets while in flight creates an ecological disturbance in the atmosphere out of all proportion to the flush itself.

A snowballing effect occurs. As these foreign bodies tumble down through the super-cooled strata, the whole moisture content of the upper air in thrown out of kilter. Woe betide those areas lying directly beneath heavily-travelled air routes.

Constant blizzards ensue. Then, because the upper air has been drained of much of its moisture it flows downward to create unnaturally low temperatures at ground level. Hence those heavy frosts.

"Ah, ha!" you exclaim. "I am beginning to see the sense of this scientific theory now. Here, without doubt, is the explanation for our worsening winters in Newfoundland!"

For, you see, we are sitting under one of the most heavily-travelled air routes in the world – the North Atlantic East West Route as it is commonly known.

The whole Island comes under the direct influence of the man-made precipitation which occurs in conjunction with this route. But the zone of greatest intensity lies in a hundred-mile wide zone centered between Gander and Corner Brook.

Those who wonder why more precipitation falls out of the sky and lingers on the ground don't have to look far for the answer. But they had better not look up. Some of the new jumbo jets have eighteen flush toilets apiece.

With the great increase in air travel in recent years, allied with the heavier menus being offered in tourist and first class alike, is it any wonder we have come through one of the worst winters in living memory?

International law is involved here, of course. But it is no good for any or all of our Members to get up in the House of Commons and demand that the airlines of the world stop flushing their toilets on Newfoundland and mucking up our weather.

These matters are never that simple. Look what a wrangle it took to get the two hundred mile limit idea in. We will have to "batten down the hatches" as it were and take it on the chin while they battle it out in the law courts of the world.

Moral law, if nothing else, is on our side. I mean, if the good Lord had intended man to flush toilets whilst five miles up in the air, He would have built Mount Everest complete with a crapper at the top.

Of course, when the general public gets hold of the news there'll be no stopping popular demonstrations. We can foresee something along the lines of the rebellious colonists in America who took as their motto: "Don't tread on me."

Other countries don't put up with it so why should we? You don't hear tell of worsening winters in other parts. No, in fact I wouldn't be surprisd if the airlines have an anti-flush pact with those bigger nations. Might makes right in the world today.

What retaliatory measures we can take if talks break down remains to be seen. We could probably drop a few of our politicians on the home countries of offending airlines, but then the International Red Cross would raise a hue and cry about inhumane tactics and terror weapons. The road ahead is long and steep. It may be years before we see flushing in Newfoundland skies restricted and the troubled air returned to its natural state.

But it is worth it to get back those milder winters again where there is just as much mud, fog and rain in February as there is in July. It is a state devoutly to be wished.

"When the Lights Go on Again" as Vera Lynn used to sing during the last war, "...and rain or snow is all, that will fall from the skies above." No longer will the peasant in the fields glance upward with apprehension at the distant roar of an Air Canada DC-9.

No longer will the humble fisher secure hatches and duck below at the overhead approach of the night flight from Boston to Prestwick. We'll be back to normal precipitation again: that is to say, a steady drizzle from January to December.

There'll be no more of those climatic extremes such as we have endured this winter. Without artificial "seeding" of the atmosphere by those airborn waterclosets the clouds will release their noisture content in a controlled fashion and the cheerful notation of R-D-F will be seen once more in our weather forecasts.

Now that the full story is out I am sure that every patriotic Newfoundlander will be prepared to do his bit – and do it, if we fail to get a flushing halt by civilized means, in the skies over Montreal, New York, London, et cetera.

We have the advantage of superior weaponry and if it comes to that we're prepared to flush them right back into the ice age!

159

Flying in the Face of Nature

On Saturday I was overcome by stark, raving pique.

Tether's end, bottom of endurance, limit of patience and all that.

Going berserk is never pretty. The consequences can be grave. But I did it and I'm glad!

Saturday was May 19. It was also filthy cold with an icy drizzle in spots. Like just about every bleeding day in May so far.

Well past the middle of the month and not so much as a paltry dandelion peeped up yet. Frost every night and a five-degree heat wave every day. It is beyond reason.

I was out in the country at the time. Frigid blasts were coming up the hill from the sea and a flock of crows went past hacking and coughing their heads off. It looked like snow again.

It was then that something snapped and I pitched into a frenzy of outrage.

Leaping from my conveyance, I flung off a heavy, soggy sort of garment that has seldom been off my back, night or day, since last November.

I stepped, lightly clad, into the stinging gale.

"OK, damn it!" I thought in a rage, plucking out my shirt tails and whacking open my collars. "Whistle in through here if that's the way you want it!"

160

At that stage there was no holding me. I raced off a little distance and commenced jumping up and down in a frosted puddle until both feet were thoroughly soaked. Then I hove myself down on the chill turf and pretended to be sunning myself.

By Sunday night I was handy about dead.

Some say it is a more serious case if the cold strikes up through you; others hold that down is the more perilous direction.

But when the chill enters your fragile carcass from both ends at once and joins up somewhere in about the middle of your poor person, the results can be spectacular.

For a start, the digestive tract is short-circuited. Add to that delicate condition a racking cough and you're kept constantly on your toes. Then there's the nose running, too.

The pounding head, the sore throat, the fearsome cramps, the nasty back, the stinging eyeballs...oh, death, where is thy sting?

Monday was more or less a merciful blank to me. I remember once attempting to introduce my gurgling guts to a cup of hot chicken soup, but that substance was rejected at an astonishing rate of knots.

A few aspirin tablets as advised by the physicians got caught up somewhere down the chute and a bit of novelty was interposed into the game when I spent the next two hours actually sneezing them back up.

From past experience I knew that an application of medicinal brandy was useless except you have a bumper supply on hand and stick into it ravenously until either yourself or the flu has given up the ghost.

But a hangover, however slight, on top of influenza, leaves no other course open to you but self-destruction.

All in all, it was a futile gesture. Flying in the face of nature – however desperate the situation – leads only to rack and ruin.

On First Looking into Summers' Lesson Book

It went through me like a shot.

I am hardly got the better of it yet even though it happened the evening before last. Where in the world is our education system headed? We are come to a pretty pass when youngsters' heads are being pumped full of such stuff!

Where is the Ministry of Education while all this is going on? Is there some sinister plot behind all this which must be got to the bottom of? A Royal Commission is called for, no later than today.

Anyway, all this came about as I settled down the other evening to read a school book. Yes, an innocent little lesson book. I was in perfectly good spirits up 'til then.

The book *Geography of Newfoundland* for grade fivers, was sent along to me by the authors, Summers and Summers, a local couple residing in Beachy Cove.

An admirable book (as I then thought) and proof that the youngsters today are getting at least some grounding in the nature of their own Country.

Instuctional. Educational. Enlightening. I noted there was much of interest as I leafed through preparatory to reading it. Yes, a step in the right direction. Splendid pictures, et cetera.

Then, as happened so, the volume fell open to page 12. On it there is a map of this Country including Labrador. It was then that the full heft of the outrage struck me.

There, in big letters...PLACENSIA BAY!

There! How do you like that! PLACENSIA BAY! The like of it being left on the market! The like of it being drilled into youngsters' heads!

How can they possibly explain such a scandalous and gross error?

They spelled "Michikamau" right. They hit "Ossokmanuan" right on the button. All outlandish names up in Labrador.

True, there are a few other spelling errors on that map, but they are trifling. "Port-aux-Basque", for instance, although some might say it was high time someone kicked the "S" out of Port-aux-Basques.

Or "Grosswaser Bay" up north. And, of course, Sin John's is often spelled wrong these days.

All minor points. But how anything professing to be a geography of Newfoundland can be put on the market and into the schools when they can't even spell the name of the most benevolent, most distinguished, most noble body of water the hand of the Creator placed upon the face of the earth is beyond me!

This, a *Geography of Newfoundland*? When the chiefest, most grandest, most splendid geographical feature on it can't be got right? Phaugh, Sir, don't make me laugh!

As I said, coming across the like of this right out of the blue turned my blood. I haven't been the same since. It took the good right out of me.

Why is this fatally-flawed book not scrapped immediately? Why hasn't it been recalled? If a high sheriff's warrant does not go out on the instant then bandages should be tied over the youngsters' eyes to keep the scandal from them.

As you might imagine, I was in a hostile mood for reviewing Summers and Summers further. Foul sorts. Then, as usual, I was softened by the lights of Christian charity and tried to make allowances.

Perhaps, I reasoned, they caught their grievous mistake too late to fix. Maybe, I thought, the magnitude of their error will cause them to try to make it up to that Far Greater Bay in later pages.

Right here, for instance, in this chapter entitled "A Raindrop's Story."

163

I dare say they'll dwell on this Country's most outstanding feature, namely, Placentia Bay, right here.

What they do is, you see, they have their raindrop going around all over the place, down in the ocean one minute, up in the clouds when the sun draws water, pitching down here and there the length of the Country.

This particular raindrop has got speech so he is able to tell us about all the places he passes through. It is all calculated to catch and hold the juvenile interest. Neatly done, I must say.

He first comes along by Fogo Island. "Ah, ha," says our rambling raindrop, "when we passed Cape Bonavista the ice began to break up and much of it melted and became part of the ocean."

He's not much of a one to tell a yarn as he doesn't drag it out enough. Little more than mentions the names of the places he's pitching on or travelling past. On down along Cape Race and Burgeo, then up to Stephenville Crossing and Howley.

"One day the sun shone bright (he's on the Grand Banks, now) and evaporated me back into the air. I passed over the Avalon Peninsula...."

Hang on. Here it comes. He's not going to have half a yarn, you think, about the time he hauled around Cape St. Mary's or pitched down in Piper's Hole! No, poor hand!

"I passed over the Avalon Peninsula as far as Dildo, in Trinity Bay," he continued dryly, "and then I passed over Trinity Bay (yes, old man, a jolly good bay to pass over, too) by way of Heart's Content and Old Perlican and so out to the open sea again."

What's this, old man? You're striking off a wrong course there aren't you? What's all this beating around the bush? You're taking up a lot of the youngsters' time by not heading for That Far Greater Bay straight away. That's what we're all interested in.

A little chop I had in the pan for supper started to burn on the stove. Being so caught up in the story I paid no heed to it. But do you know something?

That stunned raindrop must have pitched down on or passed over every spot on the island of Newfoundland but never got around to Placentia Bay! Could you credit it!

I read the chapter through and through. He's rummaging around everywhere like the raven but never a mention of the chief attraction of all. I was fit to be tied when this mawmouth is bragging about all the places he has been into and ends up..."Right now I am a tiny drop on your windowpane."

While not putting much dependence in a book that could make two gross mistakes in a row, I was foolish enough to haul back the curtain and look out. Sure enough. There he was.

"Hop the hell off that, you!" I cried hotly, rapping to the window. "Pack your traps and ship out. Don't come shagging around here if you're too nice to pitch down in Placentia Bay!"

That cowed him. The wind struck around the corner from the direction of Mrs. Tucker's and he was off like the devil through the long grass.

Good luck to bad rubbish. Devil's own boo-bagger. Hope he spends the next fifty years passing through Liberal kidneys.

By this time I was breathing heavy and all flushed. It is seldom I lose my temper like that but flesh and blood can only stand so much.

My only hope now is that there might be, as should be, a companion volume that goes along with the Summers and Summers *Geography of Newfoundland* and devoted entirely to That Far Greater Bay.

Hair

It is nothing short of surprising the rate at which fashions change in this modern age. I had it brought home sharply to me this present week.

Not too long ago a chap with long hair was looked at askance on the public streets. Now, of course, bank managers and magistrates sport curls down to their collars.

School teachers and chartered accountants cultivate mutton chops that would put the late Prince Consort in the shade. Even your political leaders and your managing editors are all a'bristle in the most debonair way imaginable.

Hair, it seems, is now the thing. A few years ago it was only the scattered violin player or the callow Bohemian youth who ran around in ringlets. But the fashion caught on in no time.

Almost any stretch of sidewalk looks like the international Old English Sheepdog trials. You see a large bush coming toward you and you expect someone to jump out from behind it and say "Boo!" They can't. They're attached to it.

As you may have gathered, I have never given much thought to my personal appearance. When I first saw what I had to work with I gave it up for a bad job. Nothing would have helped anyway, short of a complete transplant of everything above the ankles.

So far forth as hair is concerned, I found it economical in years past to get it all mowed down, smack smooth, in what was called in those far off times a "brushcut". Then I would let it all grow out again.

By this means, I was able to get by on two haircuts a year. Apart from the savings gained, it was an interesting process. It was an education in itself to watch those two yearly crops grow and come to maturity.

Those first delicate sprouts of spring, watered by the gentle rain, nourished by regular applications of Vitalis, carefully mulched with Brilliantine, invigorated by the summer sun. Then, in the fullness of time, came the harvest.

Another brushcut and the cycle of nature began again. What need for boredom, what room for ennui with a full crop always under cultivation immediately above. Many's the time I have sat for hours and watched it grow.

These past few years, however, it has been more than your face is worth to get a brushcut. You would be mocked and jeered in the marketplace. But just how far the pendulum had swung I didn't know until Saturday.

It was about time for another harvest. The weeds had been kept down nicely but I feared that in the case of an attack of cutleaf beetles the whole crop might be wiped out. So I went along to the barber.

"I'd like it rather on the short side, my man," I said. "Cut close on the back and sides and watch out for the rocks in the mower. Heh, heh, heh."

I always make it a point, upon settling into the chair, to pass a few such pleasantries with the barber. It puts me at ease. When you go along only a few times a year you don't get to know these lads on a first name basis.

And the idea of a stranger standing behind you with a straight razor held six inches from your throat does tend to bring out a touch of the old paranoia. Jack the Ripper might have escaped and tied up the real barber in the back room for all you know.

But after passing a few words with him, and failing to note any sinister movements, I am able to settle back and relax and let him go to it. But we digress.

This particular barber must have been overjoyed at my instructions. I dare say they took him back to the good old days. In present times, with long hair the rage, barbers have to practise on Yorkshire terriers just to keep in shape.

Anyhow, he took to the job like a starving man taking to a sirloin steak. There weren't many hairs out of place by the time he had finished, I can tell you. Rather fetching considering the material, I thought.

Oh, it wasn't a brushcut by any means. Not at all. Just an ordinary plain and simple haircut suited to the summer months and which would allow Hallowe'en to come and go before I had to undertake a similar expense again. Or so I thought.

I had no sooner stepped outside the door into the street when I started getting sharp glances. Some people were even turning around to get a second look. A few giggles broke out here and there.

When I got a chance, I glanced down and was relieved to find that the trouble did not lie in that region. Everything secured. My memory for these small but important details is not what it was.

They were obviously taking umbrage at the length of my hair. Four youths stood directly in my path, their locks down to their shoulders. I decided to put on a bold front and indicate by some means that despite the state of my head I was one of the beautiful people, like even unto them.

So I broke into a snatch of something I considered appropriate ...a tune which I believe is still popular. "Adolph Hitler's beeyouteeful in his own way; Terminal acne's beeyouteeful in its own way..." and so on and so forth.

However, it made little difference to them. The stoutest among them, a chap standing six-foot-two with a coiffure like that of Rita Hayworth in the early 1940s, jostled me rudely as I passed.

"Yaaa, yaaa, sissy!" cried the one with the Prince Valiant. "You some kind of creep running around with your hair like that?"

I had occasion to visit the bank but found conditions little better there. It was surly and suspicious looks all round and the manager, sporting Ben Cartwright muttonchops down to his collars, stood ready to lunge at the alarm bell the minute I made my move.

One of the tellers served me but with obvious distaste. The whole establishment was on edge. I distinctly heard one of the girls mutter something about "..escaped from Salmonier."

It was a relief to be outside again. But the disparaging remarks continued. "Disgusting!" "Should be horsewhipped walking around in public like that!" "The world is gone mad!" Et cetera, et cetera.

As I came abreast of a little old lady in front of the Court House steps she gave me a nasty cut across the quarters with her umbrella which, furtunately, was furled.

"Go home for shame's sake, you short-haired weirdo!" she cried, winding up for another drive down the fairway. "You're nothing but a disgrace to the parents what reared ye!"

As, indeed, I soon found out I was. That evening I dropped in on the folks and although their colours rose the minute I darkened the door, they said nothing right away. It all came to a head, as usual, at the supper table.

"By God, if I didn't think it would come to this sooner or later," declared one of them. "That crowd you been hanging around with. A bloody disgrace. Them two ears sticking out naked as the day you were born. Not enough hair on your head to hide your shirt collars, let alone cover your shoulders."

The other parent said nothing, but sobbed softly. I received orders not to set foot in the house again until it grew back to a decent length. I walked off into the sunset. They might have known when they had me that they'd have a hard row to hoe.

It was even worse at the office. The minute I stepped into the newsroom the sanitary maintenance engineer passed some clever remarks to the teletype girls and there were snickers all round. The city editor glowered at me from under his tousled locks.

When the message came that the managing editor wanted a few words with me I knew I was in for it. I waited for him in his office admiring the "Lukey's Boat" pinups on the wall. When he arrived I took the appropriate stance...eyes on low beam, hands behind back, toe digging into the carpet.

"This is a newsroom, we know, but it is also, in a way, a business office," he said. "We have all sorts of people coming and going here and even making allowances for your...ahem...artistic temperament we must keep in mind the overall impression our visitors receive.

"The business office is no place for short hair. It looks untidy and unprofessional and besides that it's dangerous. You could get your ears caught in the typewriter keys. I suggest you either buy a wig or stay home until it grows to a decent length."

So here I am confined to my place of residence knocking out bits on my portable typewriter. It isn't so bad once you get used to being

169

shunned and avoided. But I fear the electricity bill is going to be heavy.

I have to keep the lights on all day since the blinds are tightly closed. The neighbours complained that my short hair was setting a bad example for their youngsters.

At the rate fashions change these days, I may not have to stay here long. Short hair may be catching on again. Yesterday, while peeking from behind the blinds, I noticed two avant garde college students going past with their tresses shorn.

Of course, by the time short hair becomes the rage mine will be too long to qualify and still too short to squander two dollars on at the barber shop. So you see my situation.

The old saying is true: "Better to be born stylish than rich."

I'll settle for either one.

Welcome, Happy Morning!

Anticipation and preparation are often the most memorable parts of
a celebration.

There we were about to celebrate the twenty-fifth anniversary of
our Country's joining up with Canada. A committee had been struck
to plan the whole riotous affair, and a decree had gone out that all
the Country should participate.

Anxious, as ever, to keep a finger on the public pulse, I got aboard
my motorcar and drove out to see how the "Confederation Jubilee"
preparations were coming along in the rural districts.

If the frenzy of joy generated in St. John's was anything to go
by, I expected the rustical areas to be going right on end.

My investigations took me to the quaint yet thriving community
of Little Scummy Cove East, G.D. Bay, and I entered the gates of that
historic hamlet at eleven o'clock in the morning.

At first glance the prospect was surprising. I had expected the
orgy of jubilation to be in full swing. Such did not appear to be the case.

"Oh, well," I thought, "I suppose they're hanging off on the triumphal
arches until the frost is out of the ground.

"And no doubt the processional banners will be whacked up in
a precious quick hurry the minute the weather turns."

It was my aim to enter into conversation with several citizens of the place and so gauge the heights to which ecstasy had soared to date.

But it is a common fault of us journalistic chaps, when we go out from the Big City on investigational forays into the rustical districts, to trail clouds of cynicism and a skeptical nature with us.

On this occasion, I resolved to conquer that fault. I was determined to subdue any such inclination and to enter completely into the spirit of the place so as to soak up, without prejudice, the true feeling of jubilation and celebration as I found it.

I drew my conveyance to a stop in front of the main shopping mall of Little Scummy Cove East. There were some cases of empty soft drink bottles outside it and it also served as the community post office. I entered.

Or, rather, wishing to blend into the scene of riotous jubilation, I burst in.

"Confederay-SHUN! Confederay-SHUN! Confederay-SHUN! I whooped in a sort of improvised little song. "Hail to Nineteen Forty Nine! Whoo Hoo! Our side best!"

At the same time I was demonstrating a few dance steps in the middle of the shop floor although, to be sure, it was not up to Nureyev's standards as I am fallen a bit into flesh and was wearing skidoo boots at the time. But the spirit was in it.

"Good day, all! Good day, all! Good day, all!" I chortled. "By God, I don't see how we can wait until the stroke of midnight, 31 March before letting her rip!"

There was one woman with a bandanna on over at the shelves. She emitted a strangled little cry and let a bottle of sweet mustard pickles fall to the floor.

Behind the counter, the shopkeeper had been slicing off bologna. He sprang back several feet against the cash drawer and brought his knife up at the ready like a Coldstream Guards officer taking the salute.

"Well, well, well, good people," I continued in a cheery and buoyant fashion, "it won't be long now, eh, before the joy-bells ring out!

"I expect Little Scummy Cove East is right in the thick of it already! Yes, sir, I see by the schedule where this very community has been honoured as the site of the Yukon State Banquet! I expect all is agog and ago here already."

The shopkeeper backed even closer, if possible, against the cash drawer. Still holding up his bologna slicer he had managed to reach down and gain a purchase on a large beach rock used to keep the lid on the riblets barrel secured against the cat.

He was making strange faces over his shoulder and sort of hissing without moving his lips to a lady in the background who had been cutting off some yards of oilcloth.

"Mounties! Mounties!" he seemed to be telling her. "Phone! Phone!"

At this the lady made an extraordinarily quick scuttle toward a door in the back. Meanwhile, the woman customer in the bandanna had grabbed one small infant unto her bosom, snatched another by the hand and was out the door in a flash, unnaturally pale in the face.

"Oh, no doubt, sir," I said, a trifle puzzled but still cognizant of the underlying feeling of Jubilee gaiety in it all. "No doubt at all about that. That grand Mounted Police Force will be playing a key role in the celebrations throughout the year!"

"Come one step closer," remarked the shopkeeper, his voice oddly lowered, "and I'll cut your throat just so quick as I'd look at you. Yes, quicker!"

"Oh," I replied. "Yes. Um Humm. I see. Yes."

The thought flashed through my mind for the moment that these several good folk of Little Scummy Cove East had been in the midst of rehearsing a historical tableau, or something, as part of their contribution to the joyous year.

Perhaps, I supposed, on the instant, they were all so caught up in the project that they found it hard to step out of character on short notice.

Then, as I noticed a festal sunbeam glancing off the blade of the unwavering bologna-slicing implement, another thought occurred to me.

It seemed incredible but perhaps the work of the coordination committee had not penetrated this far into the rustical districts yet.

Perhaps the folk of Little Scummy Cove East had not yet been apprised of the wave of jubilation and festivity which was soon to wash over the country.

In which case, I thought with some consternation, these people must have taken me for a drug-crazed hippie or worse!

"Well, damned nice meeting you, sir," I said, edging crab-fashion toward the door. "Damned nice. It will all be made plain to you later. Wouldn't trouble the Mounties. Guess they're busy enough with the traffic tickets!"

For once, thank God, I had no trouble with the throttle baulking. There was a bit of gravel hit the clapboards but not enough to speak of.

173

The Tourists Are Coming!
The Tourists Are Coming!

A few words addressed directly to the prospective visitor to these Shores on the subject: "Largee, they says we talks quare."

Suppose you are visiting an outharbour house and are chatting with the housewife when she leaves you for a moment to see to something in the pantry or the porch. Suddenly there is a small commotion, the stamp of a foot, and the loud exclamation: "Kiss! Kiss! Kiss! Garrt!"

Needless to say, you are taken aback. You may be puzzled and even troubled. Has she suddenly gone mad? Have her passions overtopped her? You are uneasy, and that is what we seek to prevent.

Relax, for in fact she has merely found tom-oh (male cat) chewing the tail of a fish she had for supper. You must remember that what suits upalong cats does not suit Newfoundland cats. They are clever, but not bilingual like federal civil servants.

If you were to say "scat" or something similar he would probably just sit and blink at you. You must say "Kiss! Kiss! Kiss!" because that is what he has been reared on. And, of course, "Garrt!" is simply the contraction for "Get out of that!"

The field is a broad one indeed, and we can hope to no more

than skim the top and at random. There are wide differences in each area and St. John's itself is rather foreign ground to the author.

But we will touch on the usage in some outharbours. Even there you will find that what works in one place is not the thing for another community a few miles distant.

Remember "Goodbye". It is a contraction in which, over the centuries, a whole sentence has been boiled down into one word. "God be with ye" has become "Goodbye". It may be helpful to remember that contractions are often used in Newfoundland.

For example. A kindly outharbour fisherman has agreed to take the visiting mainland couple for a trip in his boat. As you get aboard he may say: "Now, sir, you can sit up in the headuver and, ma'am, you can sit back in the arsuver."

Here are two unfamiliar words. They are technical terms much used in Newfoundland marine circles. The first refers to the front or pointy end of the boat, and the other refers to the back or blunt end. See how easy it is once you get the hang of it?

To further illustrate. The shortest Newfoundland conversation is well known. It occurred when one fisherman met another on the way back from the fishing grounds. The first asked: "Arn?" To which the other replied: "Narn."

This translates as "Ever the one?" and "Never the one [fish]." Or you may hear "Never the one haypert," and wonder what a haypert is. The author has been hearing it all his life, but only last fall did he discover that it is spelled "half penny worth." He had also been taught that a certain rock in the bay was the "Jasmin" until he recently saw it spelled on the charts, "the Jerseyman."

It is a tricky business. If you stop in an outharbour and ask where the general store is located, to be told that it is "Up War Jay Lies" may head you up in the direction of the cemetry not knowing that it is really "Up towards Eli's."

Even finding your way around can be a mysterious business. The place names are odd enough, but the pronunciation has little to do with the spelling. "Sinjawns" may be easy. It is the largest city on the Awlin.

You may find your way to Bull Awl because you can take the furry across the Tickle and view the mines, although they closed down a few years ago. If you come to the Awlin (of Newfunlan) on the Gulf Furry you'll land at our rocky western gateway, Poor Bast.

175

From there you can go by road as far north as Nant Knee where the Grum Full Mission is located, or you can come east toward Sinjawns. Be sure to stop on the way to see Turn Over Park, and you may want to detour south and see Gramank and Fertchen. You probably heard that they're drilling for awl on the Gramanks?

Other places to visit are Clernvo, Turnsvo, Gamble, Fogul and Arizire. They occur on the map as Clarenville, Terrenceville, Gambo, Fogo and Heart's Desire.

About the best time to visit the Awlin is in June when the dumbledores is buzzin' around the pissabeds, or as they would say upalong where the language has been watered down to a shocking extent, "when the bees are buzzing around the dandelions."

The tourist bureau has got out a booklet which will help you to tell the difference between tuckamores and tickleaces, gowithy and crunnicks, starrigans and ballycaters.

There are also many rare species of fauna here on the Awlin. If you would like to see some in captivity just ask someone in Sinjawns to show you the way to the House. There you can view some splendid specimens of sleeveens, angishores, blackguards, merrybegots and saucy streels.

A picnic is known as a Ball Up. Don't forget the prog bag (picnic basket) and if a native asks you if you can ball the kittle be sure to play along and say yes. He will then say: "Don't be so fullish. You can't ball a kittle! You balls the water wass *IN* the kittle! Har, har, har." It is a small but traditional joke.

Older men in a place are often referred to as "Uncle." They may be no relation to the speaker. It is an honourary title. "Aunt" is used in the same way. But you won't encounter ants when you go out for a Ball Up. They may look like ants, but they are really emmets. A common unit of measurement is "Bout the same size of a emmet's egg."

A Newfoundlander when mildly excited uses the curious expression "Largee!" If he is mildly vexed he exclaims "Beda Largee!" And if he is really furious it becomes "Beda Lar Liffin Gee!" It is better then to stand to one side.

First when you come to the Awlin you may notice that the greetings are three-part as "Good day! Good day! Good day!" or "Come in! Come in! Come in!" The reason for this is not clear, although Edgerkated Fellers may say something about the magic of the number "three".

When it is time for you to leave the Awlin you may be surprised to see the women "half on a bawl" as they call it, and the men wringing your hand and shaking their heads and looking very serious. But you will be back Christmas or next year. So why?

Edgerkated Fellers haven't studied this much but it is because Newfoundlanders have a weak conception of past and future time. The past is a vague storyland of "years ago" and the future was never a real thing.

There is only now. It is now that you are going, and so you are as good as gone forever.

Oh. Goodbye!

This Dear and Fine Country
- Spina Sanctus

Well, we made it once again, boys!

Winter is over.

Oh, but there is still snow on the ground.

So what? It hasn't got a chance. It is living in jeopardy from day to day. We should pity it because it will soon be ready for the funeral parlour.

It is only a matter of another few paltry weeks and we shall see it disappear into brown and foaming brooks; we shall see the meadows burning green and spangled with little piss-a-beds like tiny yellow suns.

Winter is over.

Oh, but there is still ice in the water.

So what? The globe is turning and nothing can stop it. We are revolving into light.

The fisherman tars his boat on the beach and is heated by two suns, one in the sky and another reflected from the water, and the ice on the cliff behind him drips away to a poor skeleton.

It is only a matter of a few more paltry weeks and we shall see the steam rising from the ponds and from the damp ground behind the plow; we shall see the grandmother sitting out by the doorstep for a few minutes watching the cat; we shall see the small boats a'bustle, piled high with lobster pots in the bow, and the days melting further and further into the night.

Winter is over now.

Praise God and all honour to our forefathers through generations who did never foresake this dear and fine Country.